FOREWORD

I have known Tiff for the best part of a decade - as a truly great friend, a pop up cook, a restaurant goer, an all round food fiend, a mum to a family of food fanatics and of course just a tip-top home cook.

We all enjoy food, eating and all that comes with it, but Tiff, and her entire family, really enjoy food. It is totally and utterly central to their wellbeing and happiness. She just really "gets" food. As a cook who has strived, over the years, to give nothing but pleasure to those lucky enough to sit around her table, she has amassed a phenomenal amount of priceless knowledge. As a result, she consistently delivers wonderful food fit for all occasions.

This immense experience as a cook, her grasp of human nature, spritely sense of humour - and command of the English language, all play an integral role in the wonder of this book. It is a cracker, a no-brainer for any aspiring cook, student or wannabe chef. To launch into uni life without it would be to go into battle without your troops.
Don't do it - cheap ingredients cooked to a pitiful death is just not necessary!

Phil Howard
2* Michelin chef
Chef/Owner Elystan Street
Chelsea
London
phil@philchef.com

ACKNOWLEDGEMENTS

For Charlie, Eric, Harry, Josh, Milo, Malti, Max, Oli, Rob, Theo and Will...the Band of Brothers who gave me such help and encouragement. May you laugh and break bread together for the rest of your days.

Special thanks to Lisa and Catherine for persuading me to write about cookery in the first place, and to all those who read the resulting blog. To Emily, Millie and Mark for their insights on student life. To Goo for her recipe testing. To my mother and sister for never tiring of talking about food. Huge thanks to my butchers Adam, Clare, Dan and Peter at H G Walters for providing me with inspiration as well as top quality produce. And to my family Michael, Charlie and Anna...feeding such an enthusiastic audience has brought me more pleasure than I could possibly express.

And thank you for reading this book. I hope it helps you to learn to love cooking. For more food inspiration, follow me on Instagram at tiffstoptips.

Tiffany

CONTENTS

INTRODUCTION

ABOUT THIS BOOK

The aim of this book is to give you confidence in your ability to feed yourself whilst you are a student. Balls, chutzpah, get up and go...call it what you will, confidence is a transformative force that can take you to places that skill hasn't quite yet reached. Add that to an ability to read and a fondness for food and you have the perfect recipe for winning this cooking game. It is impossible to sustain life without ingesting calories so you might as well make the experience of cooking and eating them as enjoyable as possible.

I also hope that this book starts to answer the question "What goes with what?" by providing you with some pointers and encouraging your sense of adventure. Evidently you have to take into account individual taste...just because I personally abhor the thought of pineapple on a pizza does not stop thousands of them being eaten each week. And it is hard to put into words why prawn risotto is delicious but that beef risotto just doesn't work. But I hope this book inspires you to discover the combinations that taste good to you.

I hope that it also encourages a common sense, can-do attitude. Be bold. There is no better place to reinvent yourself than at university. So if you have always been the sort of person who reads a menu thinking "I won't eat this, I don't like that", now may be the time to change. A large chunk of your brain does not finish developing until you are 25, so it is not unreasonable to assume that your tastes may carry on altering until at least then, though in truth they will do so throughout your entire life. I didn't like olives until I was 29, beetroot till I was nearly 40 and I have only really had a taste for oysters recently. And I still can't stomach baked beans. But the point is to have an open mind and keep trying things.

This concise book covers the basics. If it helps to ignite an interest in cookery so much the better and then I hope that you will expand your horizons and move on to some of the fabulous cookery books on the market by Nigel Slater, Delia Smith, Jamie Oliver, Nigella Lawson and Yotam Ottolenghi, to name but a few.

ETHOS

This book assumes that for reasons of practicality - hunger, health and economy - you will have to get to grips with a kitchen, and that for many this will be a novel experience. Of course, you may be planning on getting through your entire student life with the aid of a toaster and the local take-away but if you are slightly more ambitious, read on.

For the purposes of inclusiveness, **I am going to assume a level of zero cooking ability.** That way, those of you who know more will feel pleasantly surprised, if not smug, and those of you who don't won't feel baffled. Don't be impatient if it doesn't work out how you wanted the first time around and don't be afraid to get things wrong as some of the world's greatest culinary achievements were born when things didn't quite go according to plan. The recipes in this book have been carefully chosen on the grounds that they are not needy or temperamental.

I am going to assume that you are health conscious without being obsessive. We are constantly bombarded with conflicting advice - for what it is worth mine is that protein, fruit and leafy green vegetables make us feel good and energised, but carbohydrate-stashed comfort food tastes exceptionally fine. So a lot of the latter and a little of the former will balance out your diet. Freshly prepared food is invariably healthier than the shop bought ready meal equivalent. Steamed is healthier than fried. Fat free food is often laden with sugar. Fat and salt taste really good but too much of either is not good for you. Labelling requirements mean that you should be able to find nutritional information on almost every product you buy. Read and learn.

I expect that you have ethical leanings but do not have the funds to put your money where your mouth would like to be. So fair trade and humanely reared are probably ideals to which you aspire rather than realities in your shopping baskets.

I expect that you are environmentally conscious and re-use, re-cycle and dispose of waste correctly. And if you aren't and don't, get with the programme now.

I am going to assume that you can read and follow instructions. No doubt to get to where you are now you will have combined aptitude and hard work, and so you are all going to be more than capable of producing edible food if you follow the instructions in this book.

On the other hand, I am going to assume that you are not going to do a lot of things because you just can't be arsed. So you won't be finding any instructions to sift in this book. And I have converted weight measurements to spoonfuls where possible. On the whole you can guesstimate without coming to too much harm. Most of the recipes are very forgiving and if they say two onions and you only have one it is still going to work out.

I am going to assume that you are very budget conscious.
Cooking one portion for one person is hugely expensive in terms of time and energy so I am hoping that when you find groceries on offer you have the wherewithal to freeze or store your bargains. So it is helpful to know that loose produce is invariably cheaper than prepackaged, and that special offers sometimes promise more than they actually deliver in terms of value, so do keep your eye on the ball. And beware when comparing the cost of frozen, tinned and fresh weight. To do so accurately you need to compare weight once defrosted and drained weight for cans.

I am going to presume that you have more time than you think you have. I have been intrigued that almost all of the students to whom I have spoken mentioned that they have no time. By any relative measure, students have more time than most because the vast majority have no dependants and are not bound to a workplace for 40+ hours a week. I think the real problem is actually time management, which is a bigger issue than can be squeezed into this little book. Making too much of something and freezing it for later will help anyone manage their time better...but remember to date and label what you freeze as you don't want to spend all the time you have saved trying to figure out what is in your freezer bag.

I have tried as far as possible to put myself back into my student shoes. I have tested these recipes using the same equipment that I have advised you to have and have been conscious of budget. I have given a rough indication of how many people I think a recipe will feed but as appetites vary so much it can only be a guide. Many recipes purposely over cater so that you have leftovers for another meal.

GETTING STARTED

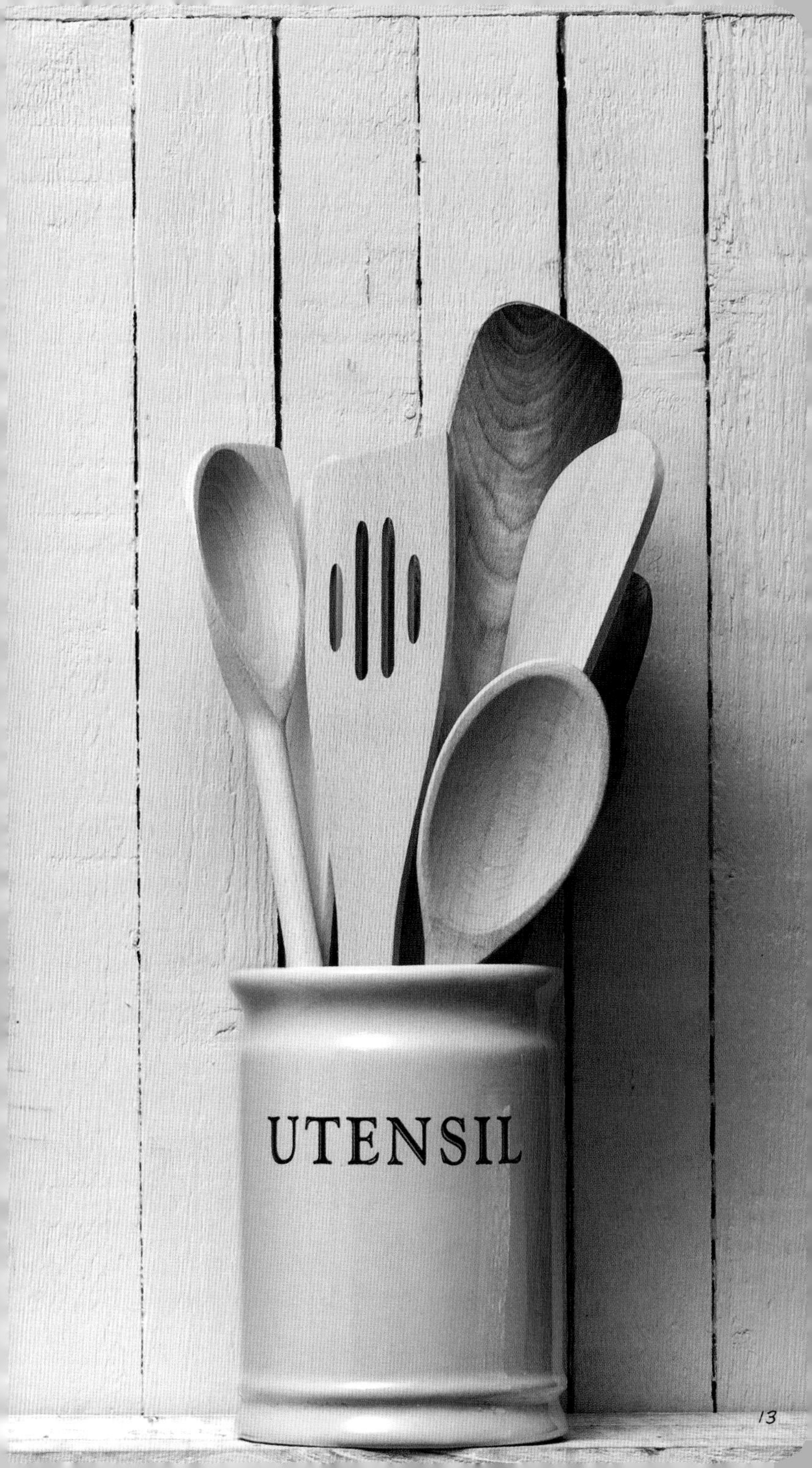
UTENSIL

KIT

I presume that you do not class kitchen equipment as a top priority. **I have listed what I consider the minimum that you can get by on; use your imagination and improvise for the rest.** I seem to remember using an ancient egg-beater as a whisk and every single saucepan to hand when a single one simply wasn't big enough.

A roll of cling film or a milk bottle make a fairly decent rolling pin, a lid can be used to drain the contents of the saucepan in place of a colander, and a fork does quite a decent job of whisking unless you are planning on making meringues.

My first mixing bowls were Tupperware containers and they were fine. In fact, it is a great idea to buy kit that is dual use...like Pyrex containers that have a plastic lid and can be used to bake in the oven or microwave, marinade, as storage or as a container to take lunch to the library.

A car boot sale is a pretty good source of inexpensive equipment (as are your parent's kitchen cupboards). That said, there are pieces of equipment that I bought at uni that I still have because they were good quality, and on the basis that I am still using them nearly 30 years later they were definitely worth the investment.

On the whole with kitchen equipment, as with many things, you get what you pay for. Quality saucepans and roasting tins for example, generally have more layers of higher grade metal and are less likely to buckle, warp and burn after prolonged use. My exception to the try and buy quality rule is the non-stick pan. Once your idiot housemate has scrubbed it with a scourer and removed the non-stick coating, not only will it no longer live up to its name but it will have become carcinogenic. So my advice here is to buy cheap and often until you can afford a better one and/or your idiot housemate moves.

One advantage of having housemates is that you can share the cost of the kit between you.

TOOLS

A 14-16 cm knife (depending on the size of you hands) and a sharpener	A dessertspoon (dsp)	Wooden or rigid silicon spoon... make sure it doesn't give way when you apply pressure to it	A mixing bowl that can double up as a serving dish
A chopping board	A sieve or a colander		A large shallow metal roasting dish (there might be one in your oven if you are lucky)
A small 2 litre 'milk' saucepan	A 24cm non-stick frying pan	A large stainless steel serving spoon	
A large 5 litre saucepan	A 26cm non-stick wok	A box grater	A smaller deep metal roasting dish, approximately 20x30cm
A ladle	Scissors	A large measuring jug	
A teaspoon (tsp)	A fish slice or rigid spatula	A vegetable peeler	An oven glove

I find it hard to manage without tongs because they give me the illusion of being more dextrous than I am and they save me from lots of burns. If you are going to invest, I would advise that it is in a pair of long slim elegant ones, not ones that have claws, as they are just annoying.

At uni, one of my housemates had a stick blender and it was brilliant for soups and sauces. The recipes in this book do not require one (apart from smoothies) but I have mentioned them where they will save you a lot of time. Blenders have also come down in price so much that many are now cheaper than stick blenders.

I am going to presume that you don't have scales. A teaspoon holds 5 ml of liquid. The dessertspoon to which I refer is the sort with which you would eat pudding and holds 10-15ml of liquid. A large serving spoon holds 40ml. If I have given you an amount in grams (g) it is because I presume that you will be able to guesstimate the weight as a fraction of a whole packet or use the guide that is printed on the packaging.

One thing that is hard for me to take into account is the efficiency or otherwise of the oven that you will be using. The timings that I have given are based on an oven that actually works, so if yours is underpowered and slow you will have to increase the times accordingly.

Talking of timing, I expect that most of you have timers on your phone...use them and you are less likely to overcook or burn food.

PRACTICAL HEALTH + SAFETY TIPS

This is a mixture of common sense and knowledge. I assume that you are not really that food hygiene aware and you do need to know some facts because food poisoning can be extremely unpleasant.

The basics are:

Wash hands before AND after handling food.

Ensure that the area of the kitchen in which you are working is clean by wiping down the surfaces.

Ensure that the utensils, boards, bowls, pots and pans you use whilst cooking are clean. I know that this sounds obvious but judging from my past experience of student kitchens, it appears to be an obscure and little understood concept.

If you are handling raw meat/fish/poultry, ensure that you wash your hands/the board/your knife before moving on to your next set of ingredients.

Wash up in hot, soapy water and use a scrubbing brush. The most efficient way to wash up is to rinse as much debris off plates/ pots etc and then fill a bowl with hot water with a small amount of washing up liquid. Scrub the dirty items until they are clean! If you have used an excessive amount of washing up liquid you may need to rinse off the suds with clean water. Be careful not to leave knives in the sink as retrieving them from the sudsy water could be painful and dangerous.

Store food that needs to be chilled in clean covered containers, or in foil, cling film or zip lock bags in the fridge. Remove unused food from tins before storing in the fridge. Food can taint other food if it is not covered, so unless you like garlic flavoured yoghurt it is best to be fastidious.

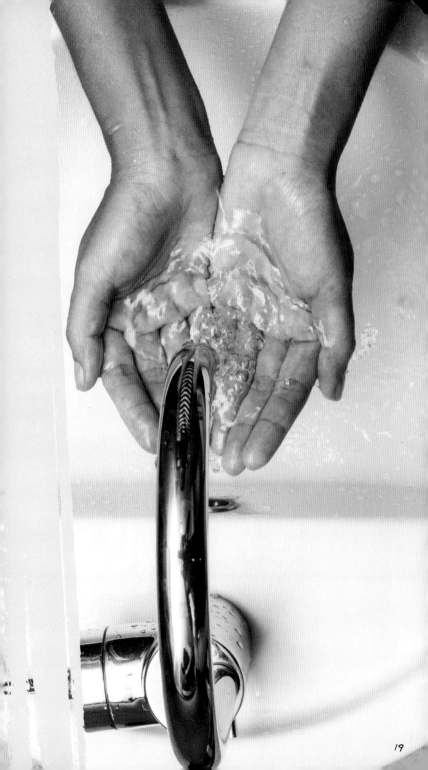

Do not put hot food into the fridge. Whilst it is important to chill food and refrigerate it as soon as is feasible, introducing something hot into a cold fridge will raise the temperature inside the fridge above a safe level -about 5 degrees- and is likely to spoil the other food in there, especially raw meat and dairy products. Bacteria thrive in warm moist areas. Extreme temperatures kill most bacteria which is why it is important to reheat food until piping hot. Food will cool down quicker if you remove it from the saucepan in which you cooked it to a large cold, shallow container.

Fruits (including tomatoes) are best stored at room temperature. Handily citrus fruits will help to ripen avocados but they will also ripen bananas quite quickly, so you may want to keep them separate. Meat should be brought back to room temperature before cooking.

Remember, if food looks, smells or tastes odd then there is probably something wrong with it and it is not worth the risk of eating it.

If you do get food poisoning, drink as much water as possible. Bananas, dry white toast and plain rice may help you on the road to recovery. Avoid eating anything acidic (tomatoes, citrus) and also avoid lactose (in dairy products) until you are better because your gut will have produced insufficient lactase, the enzyme that helps to digest lactose, whilst you had food poisoning. Coca Cola is very good for settling upset stomachs and is much more pleasant to throw up than bile, which is the nasty bitter tasting stuff created by your liver that sometimes makes a bid for freedom after repeated retching.

Safety in the kitchen is crucial as it can be a dangerous place - knives and fire are not toys. When chopping, make sure that the fingers of the hand holding the food in place are arched. That way if the knife slips, it should not chop off the end of your fingers but slide safely down the length of them. Look down at your fingers when you are about to chop - if you can see your fingernails and they look like they are being offered up as a sacrifice to the knife then you are doing it wrong.

One fifth of all accidental fires in the home are caused by deep fat frying, so you will find none of that in this book. But there are a remaining forty per cent of fires that start in the kitchen via other means, so vigilance is necessary. Do not attempt to cook whilst intoxicated. Never leave a kitchen without checking that the hobs are all off. In the event of a fire do not attempt to extinguish it unless it is safe/you are competent to do so. Never pour water on fat as it can start a fireball. Rather leave the scene of the fire, close the door, raise the alarm for others and call 999.

GLOSSARY OF TERMS + RATINGS:

Al dente	'To the tooth' in Italian, it refers to cooking vegetables, pasta and pulses so that they still have a bite to them
Baste	Preventing food being cooked in the oven or grill from drying out by spooning over cooking juices.
Blanch	Cooking (usually) green vegetables briefly in boiling water so that they still have a bite to them and then cooling them quickly (usually by plunging them in iced water) so that they stop cooking and keep their colour.
Boil	To bring a liquid 100 degrees C and maintain it at that temperature at which point bubbles will form that energetically rise to the top of the pan and pop.
Dice	The process of chopping vegetables into small even sized pieces
Dry Fry	Frying something without the addition of oil by turning it constantly on a high heat.
Flavourless oil	An oil that will not dominate the taste of the food such as sunflower, groundnut or grape seed oil.
Heaped	Means just that, you should not be able to fit any more on the spoon.
Par boil	This means to cook something only partially in boiling water. Not dissimilar to blanching but once a vegetable has been par boiled it usually needs another cooking process before it is completely cooked.
Sauté	This literally means 'jump' in French. It means cooking meat, fish or vegetables quickly in oil or butter on a brisk heat until brown.
Sealing	Used to describe the action of browning meat to 'seal' the flavour in.
Season	Almost every recipe has this instruction. It means taste the food and add salt and/or sugar in small quantities until it tastes just how you want it. Can also mean adding oils, spices, herbs.

Simmer	Similar to boiling but in fact at a temperature just below the boiling point where the bubbles formed are smaller and much more laid back, lethargic even.
Sweat	This is the process of cooking vegetables on a low heat in a small amount of fat with the lid on so that they soften without colouring.
Shred	Slicing or tearing food into fine strips
Refresh	To run cold water over food which has just been cooked in hot water to cool it down rapidly and thus prevent further cooking.

Numbers	'1X' means that although the recipe has been written for one portion it can easily be multiplied up to feed more. I have guesstimated portions based on a hearty appetite rather than a delicate one.
Timings	I have measured the approximate timings from the moment that the utensils and ingredients are assembled on the kitchen counter until the time the meal can be served. So the timings do not necessarily indicate an amount of undivided attention that you will need to devote to a recipe, as they will include oven time or marinating time. Where lengthy marinating is required I have specified that separately.
Difficulty	I asked two students to rate the recipes and they didn't come across anything that they considered too difficult, which is a relief because otherwise it shouldn't be in the book. I have tried to highlight anything that might be tricky in the main body of the recipe. Often things are simply laborious rather than tricky, such as stirring a white sauce so that it isn't lumpy. As with many things in life practice will make perfect. The more often you make something the more dextrous, efficient, confident and ultimately competent you will become.

BREAKFAST
AND
BEYOND

BREAKFAST AND BEYOND

I say 'and beyond' because you are students and inevitably keep really odd hours. So most of this section makes perfectly good supper dishes which is handy given that you may have only just woken up at what is supper time for the rest of the population.

Eggs...How To

Inexpensive, simple, quick, versatile, perfect... what is not to like other than the fact that they are very easy to get wrong? Once mastered, you will have a repertoire that makes you look like a real pro.

It will help tremendously if you buy eggs that are fresh, so do go to the very back of the shelf to find the ones that have been laid most recently. The quality of the eggs you buy is also crucial...there are some delicious free-range dark brown eggs on the market with intensely yellow yolks that taste delicious.

Because eggs cook so rapidly, dexterity and planning are key, so read the recipe thoroughly before you launch in.

Boil

Put two large fresh eggs in a small saucepan and just cover with cold water. Get the bread ready to make into toast. Get a plate ready with salt, pepper, cutlery and egg cups (a small glass stuffed with some loo roll will do in their absence). When the water is hot, put the bread in to toast. When the water starts to boil vigorously, time for 1 minute and 15 seconds. Remove the eggs from the water, lop the top off with a knife and you will have eggs with a just cooked white and a runny yolk, all ready for dippy soldiers. If you like them more well done then cook for longer: 1.45 and you will have a part liquid yolk, 2.15 a hard yolk with a soft texture and 3 minutes and you have a hard boiled egg. Remember that the eggs will carry on cooking so taking the top off them as soon as possible is important.

Poach

Do not use any of those ghastly poachers unless you want to waste your money and eat eggs that taste of rubber.

Bring a pan with water approximately 5cm deep to the boil and then turn the heat down so that the water is just simmering gently. Take two eggs and crack each of them into two separate small bowls or cups. Put on your toast/muffin. Gently tip the eggs into the water and as soon as they seem to form a shape turn the heat down to low. Butter your toast/muffin. When the white is solid (this takes about 1 minute for a solid white and runny yolk) remove the eggs from the water with a spoon (slotted is easiest) and drain the egg on kitchen paper and then place on plate/toast/muffin, etc. You do need to be a bit dextrous to suss this one but practice will make perfect.
If your eggs aren't very fresh it will help them keep their shape if you whisk the water with a fork just before tipping the eggs into the pan.

Scramble

I firmly believe that the key to perfectly scrambled eggs is agonising slowness. Tantric eggs if you like. Crack three eggs into a bowl and whisk gently with a fork and season with salt and pepper. Melt a generous knob of butter in a small non-stick pan on the lowest heat possible. Once the butter has melted, tip the eggs into the pan. Stir gently and occasionally, easing the cooked egg off the surface of the pan until they reach the desired consistency. During this time, toast your bread or bagel. At the risk of stating the obvious, the fewer the eggs in the pan the shorter the time it will take but it all depends on the surface area of your pan.

Fry

In a non-stick pan, crack an egg or two into either melted butter or warmed oil, or a mixture of both. Not too much, you aren't trying to teach the egg to swim. Season the egg yolk with a pinch of salt and a grinding of black pepper. When the egg white has turned from translucent to white your egg should be ready. Ease out with a slotted fish slice or spatula and eat.

Omelettes

Omelettes are not difficult when you know how and once mastered will become a delicious, satisfying and speedy option. A 20cm non-stick frying pan will make a 3 or 4 egg omelette. I crack the eggs into a jug or bowl, break them up gently, season them with salt and pepper and then add a variety of flavours or what is to hand. Fresh herbs, especially snipped up chives, work well. Cheese, ham or mushrooms are all fairly classic. I like goat's cheese because it is very light in comparison to say a hard cheese like Gruyere or Cheddar. Anything that is on the heavy side is best added at the end of cooking.

Before you start cooking you need to have all your ingredients ready because the whole process is very rapid. So have the cheese grated finely or the ham sliced or the mushrooms sautéed. You can cook them in the same pan before removing them to a bowl to save on washing up.

Heat the pan for a few minutes then add a knob of butter to the hot pan - not so hot that it burns, but that the butter foams. Tip in the egg mixture and using a palette knife (or a spoon if you don't have one) push the edges into the centre allowing the uncooked egg to escape to the edge of the pan and gently keep repeating the process. Much depends on how runny or not you like your eggs (very in my case) but remember that when you fold the omelette over it will carry on cooking for a bit so when you decide to do the folding thing the omelette should look slightly less cooked than you actually want.

So when there is barely any liquid egg left, scatter on your chosen flavouring, take a deep breath and go for the fold. In two is easier - you tip half the omelette onto the plate and then flap over the other half on top of it. If you are feeling dextrous go for the thirds. Tip a third of the omelette over to the centre with a knife or spatula, tip that onto the plate and then the other side folds on top of that.

It takes a lot longer to read (and write) the recipe than to make the omelette!

FRITTATA

I have a friend who can only cook one thing and this is it, so it really can't be that difficult. It is a superb use of leftovers, and will result in a quick and substantial meal.

Serves: 4

Cooking: 20 mins

Difficulty: Medium

INGREDIENTS

An onion, chopped

3 or 4 small boiled and cubed potatoes

Pepper...any colour, deseeded and chopped

Bacon/chorizo/sausage, chopped into bite-sized pieces

Cheese, a large palmful, grated

6 eggs, cracked into a bowl, gently whisked and seasoned with salt and pepper

HOW TO MAKE IT

Turn on the grill to high. In your non-stick frying pan melt a dessertspoon of butter with a similar amount of olive oil and throw in the onion. Keep stirring until it has softened then add the potato followed by the sausage, bacon or chorizo. When all are cooked, tip on the eggs.

Do not stir. Allow a base to form, sprinkle over the cheese and then place the entire pan (with the exception of the handle, especially if it is plastic) under the grill until the egg mixture is firmish. Not rock solid, preferably with a slight wobble as the eggs will carry on cooking even after you have removed them from the heat. Put a plate larger than the diameter of the frying pan over it and invert the pan so that the frittata is on the plate ready to cut and serve. Delicious on its own but even nicer with a chunk of baguette.

I think that onion, potato and cheese works particularly well, or onion, potato and either bacon, chorizo or sausage. You can spice things up by using chilli peppers rather than sweet peppers. I personally don't like tomatoes with eggs but don't let that stop you adding them to the pan just before the egg.

SWEETCORN CAKES WITH AVOCADO SALSA

This is a very satisfying dish that is not run of the mill but is nevertheless straightforward. You may not have come across buttermilk before but if you look in the chiller cabinet of the dairy section in the supermarket you should find it. It is an inexpensive and low fat by-product of the butter making process. If you really can't track it down you can make your own by substituting the same amount of milk and adding the juice of half a lemon to it. Leave to stand for 10 minutes before using.

Serves: 4

Cooking: 25 mins

Difficulty: Easy

INGREDIENTS

FOR THE CAKES:

2 tsp baking powder

½ tsp bicarbonate of soda

1 tsp sugar

1/2 tsp cayenne pepper

5 heaped dsp of plain flour

2 eggs

150ml buttermilk

2 x 25g melted butter

4 spring onions, finely chopped

325g can of sweetcorn, drained

Half a small bunch of coriander, finely chopped

HOW TO MAKE IT

Pre-heat the oven to 180°C and put a roasting dish/baking sheet in it. Melt 25g of butter in a non-stick frying pan and pour into a bowl containing all the other ingredients except the spring onion, corn and the coriander. Stir gently until you have a batter-like consistency. Melt another 25g butter and very gently cook the spring onion until soft. Once cooked, tilt the pan to one side to drain the butter.

In the meantime, make the salsa. I have two very nasty scars to prove that trying to chop things in your hand is an exceedingly stupid idea. Avocados are a prime culprit for this idiotic method, probably because they fit in the palm of your hand more easily than they sit on a chopping board and their ripe flesh is so yielding. So I have come up with a method that is safe as well as efficient. Cut the avocado in half on the board. Remove the stone by securing it with the edge of the knife pointing away from you and easing it out of the avocado. Rest the avocado skin side down on a board. Score horizontal line 5mm apart across the flesh, then vertical

FOR THE SALSA:

2 ripe avocados, diced

1 red chilli

Juice of half a lemon or lime

Half a small bunch of finely chopped coriander

A pinch of salt

5mm lines down it. Scoop out the flesh with a spoon into a bowl and hey presto it is diced and you don't have to visit the suture department of you local A&E.

Add to a bowl (a different one to the bowl of batter) the avocado, lemon/lime juice, chilli, salt and coriander and stir gently to combine. Adjust the seasoning to taste.

Add the spring onions, corn and coriander to the batter and stir gently to combine. Add a splash of flavourless oil to the frying pan and when the fat is hot put serving sized dollops of the corn batter in the pan. They will spread so do not crowd them. After a few minutes check whether the underside is brown and if so flip them over so that they can cook on the other side. Once they are done transfer then to the oven whilst you cook the remaining batter. It may be necessary to add a little more butter/oil.

Once they are all cooked serve the cakes with the salsa on top.
These would also be good with smoked salmon, chicken, bacon, sausages or ham.

CRÊPES

This recipe is Delia Smith's from her Cookery Course book. This quantity will feed 2 for breakfast, so loads more for pudding. If you have any left over, wrap them in foil and store in the fridge for another day.

To the batter can be added some currants if you are feeling nostalgic for the kind of pancakes you used to eat on Shrove Tuesday.

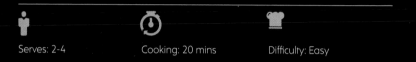

Serves: 2-4   Cooking: 20 mins   Difficulty: Easy

INGREDIENTS

6 heaped dsp plain flour

A pinch of salt

2 large eggs

200ml milk mixed with 75ml water

2 dsp melted butter

HOW TO MAKE IT

Put the flour and salt in a bowl. Whisk the other ingredients with a fork in a measuring jug and then pour over the flour and salt and whisk until there are no lumps. If you have a blender you can make the batter in that.

Warm the frying pan and when it is hot swirl around a teaspoon of butter in it. Once the butter is foaming pour in enough batter to thinly cover the base of the pan.

Once it has set and the edges of the crêpe come away easily from the pan, ease a spatula under the crêpe and flip it over. Or have a go at flipping it over without any implements and cook on the other side. Slide onto a plate; fold in half then half again. Keep warm in the oven or under foil whilst you make more. Sprinkle with caster sugar or cinnamon, squeeze over some lemon juice, whatever takes your fancy. According to my children, they are best spread with Nutella before you do the fancy fold in four trick.

AMERICAN PANCAKES

If you ask most Americans how to make pancakes they will reply 'Bisquick'. This is a flour-based powder that you can buy ready made in a supermarket to which milk and eggs are added to form a batter. But really it is easy enough to make them from scratch.

Serves: 2-4

Cooking: 20 mins

Difficulty: Easy

INGREDIENTS

2 tsp baking powder

½ tsp bicarbonate of soda

5 heaped dsp of plain flour

2 heaped dsp of caster sugar

2 eggs

150ml buttermilk (see notes on p.34)

25g melted butter

HOW TO MAKE IT

Put the dry ingredients in a bowl. Mix the liquid ingredients together in your measuring jug and then whisk the two together until all the lumps have disappeared. At this stage you can add berries, bananas, dried fruit, vanilla, cinnamon. Or not.

Heat your non-stick frying pan, dab some flavourless oil such as sunflower onto some kitchen paper and wipe the pan with it. Drop serving size spoon amounts of batter into the pan, which should fit 4 pancakes at a time. Once the pancakes start to form little craters it is time to flip them. But don't go mad and Masterchef about this otherwise you will end up clearing up a lot of batter.
Once a golden brown on each side, serve with maple syrup, fruit, butter...whipped cream with a cherry on top if you like...you decide.

PORRIDGE

Cheap, nutritious, satisfying, quick; porridge ticks all of those boxes. If you happen to be regular porridge eater, I would advise you to soak the oats in milk overnight in the fridge, in the small saucepan in which you will be cooking them. That way they cook more quickly and there is less hanging around in your cold kitchen. But they are easy enough to make from scratch.

Serves: 1X

Cooking: 10 mins

Difficulty: Easy

INGREDIENTS

3 dessertspoons oats... fine, medium, jumbo, the choice is yours

150ml milk (though if you are hardcore water works too)

Pinch of salt

HOW TO MAKE IT

Bring the milk and oats to the boil, then turn down the heat to a brisk simmer. Stir frequently until the porridge reaches the consistency that you like. Serve with more cold milk, cream, brown sugar, treacle, golden syrup, maple syrup, fresh or dried fruit.

FRENCH TOAST

French toast is the most perfect use of stale bread, though I don't remember bread getting to the stale stage at uni - but then I did live in some particularly damp and mouldy hovels.
The best bread by far is Challah (the 'C" is silent) which is a Jewish bread made with egg yolks. It is similar to brioche but with a denser texture. Failing either of those any white bread will do, but the thicker cut the better.

Serves: 1X   Cooking: 20 mins   Difficulty: Easy

INGREDIENTS

100ml milk

2 eggs

1 dessertspoon sugar

1 scant teaspoon of mixed spice or cinnamon

2-3 thick slices of stale bread

Knob of butter

HOW TO MAKE IT

Mix the first four ingredients in a shallow bowl and then put the bread in to soak. You can speed the process along by turning over the bread. The ability of the bread to absorb the liquid will depend on its level of staleness, the staler the better.

Once all the liquid had been absorbed into the bread, heat the non-stick frying pan. When it is hot throw in a knob of butter and when it starts to foam add the by now heavy bread. Check to see that it is golden brown after a few minutes and if it is, flip it over to cook on the other side.

Serve with the usual suspects...though I think that maple syrup and fruit works best.

SMOOTHIES

Now this is only going to be feasible if you have a blender of some sort. But for those who are not the breakfasting kind, this is a great way to start the day.

Serves: 1X

Cooking: 5 mins

Difficulty: Easy

INGREDIENTS

A palmful of oats

A glass of juice

Banana

Handful of frozen or fresh fruit

HOW TO MAKE IT

Blend until smooth. If you like a creamier concoction, a couple of spoonfuls of yoghurt will do the trick. And if you have a sweet tooth, add honey or maple syrup. And if you are on a muscle building bender, there are loads of revolting tasting protein powders that you can add and mask their taste with the fruit.

SNACKS – GRANOLA BARS

It may seem a bit mad to include the following recipes, but baking fever does seem to be sweeping the country. And perversely, when you are under the studying cosh it might be nice to have a brief distraction that will produce something delicious and a bit nutritious to munch on.

Makes loads

Cooking: 45 mins

Difficulty: Easy

INGREDIENTS

4 heaped large serving spoons jumbo oats

2 large serving spoons oat bran

2 heaped large serving spoons seeds (sesame, sunflower, pumpkin, chia, flax, poppy)

250g dried fruit (apricots, dates, raisins, sultanas, cherries, cranberries)

2 dsp nut butter (peanut, almond, cashew)

100g chopped nuts (almond, cashew, peanut, brazil, pistachio, macadamia, hazlenut)

4 heaped large serving spoons light muscavado sugar

10 dsp of liquid sugar - honey, agave, maple, rice malt, treacle

100g butter

1 dsp salt

HOW TO MAKE IT

These are a fabulous snack and will perk you up when you have that afternoon energy dip. A particularly good thing to have with a coffee whilst studying for exams, they will be so much more delicious than the shop bought equivalent. The downside is that the raw ingredients are far from cheap.

Melt the butter and sugars, add the dry ingredients and stir well. Spoon into a tin lined with baking parchment (I used my 20cm x 30cm roasting tin) and bake at 160°C for 30/35 minutes, until the surface is golden brown.

Leave to cool before cutting.

45

BLUEBERRY MUFFINS

Muffins are ridiculously easy to make and they freeze quite well. So if you do have a deep fairy cake tin, why not give them a go? They will have much healthier ingredients than the shop bought equivalent.

Serves: 6

Cooking: 30 mins

Difficulty: Easy

INGREDIENTS

1 very ripe mashed banana

150g wholemeal self-raising flour

50g brown sugar (I like demerara)

142ml buttermilk (see notes on p.34)

50ml flavourless vegetable oil (sunflower is good)

1 egg lightly beaten

100g frozen blueberries

HOW TO MAKE IT

Mix the mashed banana with the sugar and flour in a mixing bowl. Stir in the remaining liquid ingredients but not too much - the batter should look lumpy and as if you could have tried harder. Add in the blueberries and then spoon into either a buttered tin or into muffin liners. Bake for 20 minutes at 180°C or until a skewer/ piece of spaghetti comes out clean of wet batter when inserted into the muffin.

If you are going to freeze these, make sure you exclude as much air as possible from the bag - that way they won't get freezer burn.

BANANA BREAD

You will need a rectangular loaf tin approximately 25x 12x 7cm for this. I found one at a well-known supermarket that costs less than half a pint at a pub. If you attempt to cook it in some random vessel, just remember that the mixture will expand by about one third.

Serves: 8-10   Cooking: 45 mins   Difficulty: Easy

INGREDIENTS

125g softened butter

10 heaped dsp sugar

2 eggs

10 heaped dsp plain flour

1 tsp bicarbonate of soda

½ tsp salt

3 very ripe, mashed bananas

7 dsp buttermilk
(see notes on p.34)

1 teaspoon vanilla

HOW TO MAKE IT

Beat the butter and sugar together with a wooden spoon. Stir in the eggs followed by the dry ingredients and finally the wet ones. Pour into the buttered loaf tin and bake for 30 minutes at 180°C or until a skewer or piece of spaghetti comes out clean. Leave to cool slightly before slicing.

PASTA

PASTA

Pasta is a simple mixture of flour and eggs that it is synonymous with Italy but the fiercely regional nature of food in that country means that there are literally hundreds of types of pasta and each shape has an affinity with a specific type of sauce. For the purposes of this book we are not going to be either precious or authentic and are just going to stick to a few types. That way you won't have dozens of scrawny little packets of different shapes, insufficient for one portion and all with different cooking times. I am not a fan of supermarket fresh pasta so do what the Italians do on the whole which is to use good quality dried pasta.

Linguine is my long slim pasta of choice, but the ubiquitous spaghetti is an obvious alternative. Great for carbonara, Bolognese, puttanesca - punchy sauces that have a lot of flavour, but not too much volume. I love penne for the way the perfect amount of sauce seems to cling tenaciously to its ridges, but other 2 inch shapes such as fusilli or rigatoni are all great for sauces that are less liquid and have a bit more substance - sausage, mushroom, Genovese. I prefer a twisty shape with ridges called cavatappi to macaroni for a cheese sauce but the point here is that you choose the two or three shapes that you like best and keep them stocked in your cupboard for convenience.

As far as measurements go a standard 500g pack of pasta should feed four so just quarter the packet for a portion. For smaller shapes I use the bowl from which I am going to eat the pasta as a guide. The pasta will expand by about 1/3 and since I have used this method to judge the amount I rarely waste any pasta.

As far as how to cook pasta look no further than Italy - 'al dente' - that is only until the pasta still has a bite to it, and in water 'salato come il mare', though if global warming carries on apace, the Italians may well have to come up with a new phrase for how salty pasta water should be. Heat water in the largest saucepan you possess, and when it is boiling, throw in some salt and a glug of oil and then the pasta. Stir to ensure that it doesn't stick to each other and cook according to packet instructions. Do not overcook it, especially if it is to be put in the oven later for a further bit of baking.

If you have made some of the sauces below and frozen them, even if you don't own a microwave, you are only 20 minutes away at the most from eating a bowl of pasta from when you first walked in the door. And that's a thought as comforting as eating the pasta itself.

SIMPLE TOMATO SAUCE - MAKES A LOT

As well as being simple, nutritious and delicious, I really think that this is the single most versatile recipe in this book. You can eat it just as it is or use it for any of the variations that follow this recipe.

Makes 15 portions   Cooking: 3 hours   Difficulty: Easy

INGREDIENTS

4 roughly chopped onions

3 cloves garlic, peeled and smashed whole with the flat edge of a knife

6 dsp olive oil

3 ribs celery, chopped

8 diced carrots

2x 800g tins plum tomatoes

80g tube tomato paste

1 dsp dried oregano

1 pinch dried chilli flakes

1 Parmesan rind (this is the end of a piece of Parmesan that is too hard to eat and usually gets thrown away)

1 dsp salt

HOW TO MAKE IT

Sweat the onions in the oil on a low heat for 15 minutes but do not colour. Add the carrots, celery and garlic and continue to cook for another 45 minutes, softening without colouring. Add the chilli, salt and oregano, give a quick stir then add the tomato paste, tinned tomatoes and Parmesan rind, swilling the tins out with water to about a ¼ of the depth of the tin and adding this to the pan. Stirring occasionally, cook for a couple of hours at a low bubble, breaking up the tomatoes as you go.

Taste and season, adding salt, pepper and a pinch or two of sugar if the sweetness of the carrots and onions has not balanced out the acidity of the tomatoes. Leave to cool, remove the Parmesan rind, then liquidise if you have the means. If you do not it will still taste delicious.

This recipe yields 3 litres of sauce that I would freeze in individual packs of 200ml (about 4 large serving spoonfuls).

TOMATO SAUCE - VARIATIONS

The recipes below use 200ml of sauce and serve 1, but can easily be multiplied up to serve more. All of these ideas can be used to jazz up a jar of shop bought tomato sauce.

Tomato Sauce with Bacon
Chop a rasher or two of streaky bacon into bite size pieces, dry fry in the non-stick pan and add the tomato sauce when the bacon is cooked through. If the bacon is particularly fatty, drain the fat off prior to adding the tomato sauce.

Tomato Sauce with Sausage
Remove the casings from one or two sausages. Dry fry the sausage meat in the non-stick pan, squashing the sausage flat and breaking it up into bite size pieces so that it cooks through quicker. Drain away any fat that has leeched out of the sausage. Add the tomato sauce when the sausage is thoroughly cooked.

Tomato Sauce with Prawns
Add a handful of defrosted raw prawns to some warmed tomato sauce. When they have turned firm and pink and are thoroughly hot, they are cooked.

Tomato Sauce with Mushroom
Toss some sliced mushrooms in butter or oil. When cooked, add the tomato sauce.

Tomato and Spinach Sauce
Add some cubes of frozen leaf spinach to the tomato sauce and gently warm in a saucepan until the spinach is defrosted and the sauce is hot.

Tomato and Mascarpone Sauce
If you would like a creamier version of the tomato sauce, add a couple of dessertspoons of this soft Italian cream cheese to the sauce and heat through.

These are just a few ideas - you could add peppers, chillies, chilli oil, peas, aubergines, olives, pancetta, courgettes - use your imagination.

MACARONI CHEESE/ CHEESE SAUCE

Is there anyone out there who doesn't like this? It is one of the ultimate plates of comfort food but I have noticed that there is a myriad of different versions. For me, macaroni cheese should be quite a lot of cheese sauce and not that much macaroni. It is baked in a large shallow dish so that the sauce cannot sink to the bottom and escape from the pasta. There is a riot in my family if breadcrumbs are not sprinkled on top. This recipe will achieve all of those - if the results don't float your boat then tweak away until it does! I think that petits pois are the ideal vegetable to go with macaroni cheese.

Serves: 4

Cooking: 50 mins

Difficulty: Medium

INGREDIENTS

200g macaroni or similar shaped pasta

50g butter

4 heaped dsp plain flour

200g grated cheddar cheese

1 litre milk

Nutmeg

A handful of breadcrumbs

HOW TO MAKE IT

Cook the pasta in your largest saucepan for slightly less time than indicated on the packet so it is very al dente, and then drain. Into the pan put the butter and allow it to melt in the residual heat. Stir in the flour to the butter until it forms large amalgamated lumps. Add the milk to the pan and turn on the heat to medium. This part is crucial...keep stirring with a fork (or whisk if you happen to have one) until the large lumps of floury butter (or buttery flour) dissolve and the sauce thickens. When it doesn't appear to be thickening any more add in the cheese, a grating of nutmeg and turn off the heat. Add the pasta, stir thoroughly and transfer to a dish . Sprinkle on the breadcrumbs and bake for 20 minutes at 180°C or until the top is brown and bubbling.

Like many baked pasta dishes, macaroni cheese tastes better the second time that it is heated up and also freezes very well.

The other piece of good news on the life skills front is that you are now about a bay leaf away from making a béchamel sauce - just leave out the cheese and you are sorted.

By the way, if you ever have a lumpy sauce disaster, a stick blender or blender will sort it out. Just ensure if using a blender that the sauce is not too hot, otherwise the pressure of the steam will force the lid off, leaving you with a worse disaster than you started with - at best a heavy duty cleaning job, but at worst a visit to a burns unit.

BOLOGNESE SAUCE

BOLOGNESE SAUCE

There are so many different versions of this sauce, but I have a theory that most people's favourite recipe for Bolognese is their mother's. Just in case my theory is wrong, here is a blueprint recipe for you. The quantities are large because ground beef is frequently on a 'buy two get one free' offer and this recipe takes advantage of that for the sake of economy and convenience.

20 portions

Cooking: 3 hours

Difficulty: Easy

INGREDIENTS

3 x 450g packets of ground beef

1x 250g packet of smoked streaky bacon, finely chopped

6 onions, finely chopped

½ head celery, finely chopped

250g mushrooms, peeled and cut into small pieces, put in a large bowl

2x 400g tins plum tomatoes

140g jar tomato puree

2 dsp dried oregano

Parmesan rind

A large teaspoon of sugar or redcurrant jelly or similar

1 dsp salt

HOW TO MAKE IT

Sweat the onions in a small amount of olive oil in your largest pan with the oregano, turning over frequently to prevent sticking. It seems like quite a lot of onions but they contain a lot of water and their volume will reduce significantly. And if chopping them makes you cry, try wearing glasses and whatever you do don't rub your eyes, it won't help! After 5 minutes or so add the celery and continue stirring often. Add the bacon to the celery/onion mixture. Once the bacon is cooked, tip the entire contents of the pan into the bowl with the raw mushrooms. Pre-heat the oven to 150°C.

Now brown the beef over a moderately high heat, using no added fat as there will be plenty in the meat. Break up the meat as it browns so that no lumps are formed, spooning into the onion/celery, etc bowl when it is no longer red and raw. When the last lot of beef is browned, add the contents of the bowl back to the pan.

Now add tomatoes and purée/paste and Parmesan rind, the sugar/jelly and salt and having given the lot a thorough stirring, bring to the boil and then put in the oven. Stir every hour or so breaking up any lumps of tomato as you do. It can stay in the oven a long time...say 3 to 4 hours. The Bolognese will have cooked down and the flavour intensified.

Remove from the oven to cool and spoon off any fat that has pooled on the surface. Spoon the fat into something like an empty yoghurt pot or jar and when it is cool put it in the fridge where it will solidify. You can then put it in the food recycling bin. NEVER pour fat down the drain - the result will be a very expensive visit from a plumber. When cool, divide the Bolognese into serving size amounts. This quantity will yield about 3.5 kg or 20 x175g portions. 175g of Bolognese equates to 2 large serving spoons.

There are very few pasta shapes with which Bolognese doesn't work to eat on its own, but it can be put to other uses.

TRADITIONAL LASAGNE

Once you have made the cheese sauce, this is really just an assembly job.

Serves: 4 | Cooking: 1 hour | Difficulty: Easy

INGREDIENTS

700g Bolognese sauce

Cheese sauce (as on p.58 in the macaroni cheese recipe but with 125g mozzarella instead of the Cheddar)

12 or so lasagne sheets

HOW TO MAKE IT

In a dish approximately 30cm square, put a splash of cheese sauce on the bottom, then cover the surface of the dish with lasagne sheets. If your dish is an odd shape just break a lasagne sheet to fill in any gaps. Spread half of the Bolognese on top, followed by a couple of large serving spoonfuls of cheese sauce. Top with more lasagne sheets and repeat. Spoon over the remaining cheese sauce on top of the last layer of lasagne sheets and bake for 30 minutes at 180°C until piping hot.

As an option, you can always add in a layer of defrosted frozen leaf spinach to add colour, texture and taste to your dish, not to mention a green leafy vegetable to your diet!

Either eat immediately or divide into freezer dishes, cool and freeze.

Lasagne served with garlic bread always seems to go down particularly well and it is great with a green salad too.

CHEATS LASAGNE

A less time-consuming-to-make and lighter-to-eat version.

Serves: 4/5

Cooking: 45 mins

Difficulty: Easy

INGREDIENTS

700g Bolognese Sauce

Cheese sauce (as on p.58 in the macaroni cheese recipe but with 125g mozzarella instead of the Cheddar)

500g pasta such as fusilli or penne

HOW TO MAKE IT

Pre-heat the oven to 180°C. Cook the pasta for slightly less time than the packet instructions and drain. Stir in the Bolognese (and some spinach if desired), tip the lot into a dish and pour over the cheese sauce. If you like breadcrumbs add them now and bake for 30 minutes until piping hot and bubbling.

If you are making these in bulk to freeze individually, wait until all the components are cool before mixing them together and freezing.

CARBONARA

I always think that this is such a clever sauce. Carbonara tastes creamy but has none in it - it is a perfect emulsion of eggs, pancetta and cheese. If you buy the little packets of cubed pancetta that last for ages in the fridge, you should be able to make this quite spontaneously.

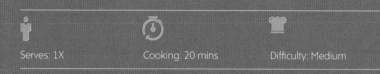

Serves: 1X   Cooking: 20 mins   Difficulty: Medium

INGREDIENTS

90g pancetta or chopped smoked streaky bacon

150g pasta

1 whole egg and one egg yolk extra

30g grated Parmesan

HOW TO MAKE IT

Bring a pan of water to the boil. Add salt and a spoonful of oil together with the pasta and set a timer for when it will be ready. Heat up your non-stick pan to dry fry the bacon/pancetta. If it is really fatty, spoon off all but one dessertspoon of the oil from the pan and if you happen to have some white wine or Vermouth (who knows, you may have had a James Bond themed party and by some miracle not been drunk dry by your mates), add a generous splash to the pan and let it bubble vigorously until there are only a couple of dessertspoons of liquid in the pan. Turn off the heat.

Whisk the eggs with nearly all the Parmesan, a grating of nutmeg and a grinding of black pepper in a small bowl. Do not add any salt at this stage because the pancetta is likely to be salty enough. Just before you drain the pasta, use a fork to whisk into this mixture a large serving spoonful of hot pasta water - as long as you whisk sufficiently this will stabilise the egg and stop it scrambling. Turn off the heat, drain the pasta and then add it to the bacon pan. Gradually pour over the egg mixture onto the pasta (rather than onto the base of the pan itself) at the same time as you stir the pasta. You should end up with silky, shiny, sauce-coated pasta rather than a curdled heap.

If you achieve the former, well done you. There is something quite sexy about being able to produce this dish so I think that it is a good bet for a date night. If the latter scrambled sauce was the result, do not lose heart, it will still taste delicious and you can keep trying until you crack it. And maybe practice before you go for the date night option.

Serve with the remaining Parmesan sprinkled over.

RAW TOMATO SAUCE

If there are some cheap ripe tomatoes around this is a fabulous sauce.

Serves: 1X

Cooking: 20 mins

Difficulty: Easy

INGREDIENTS

3 or 4 ripe tomatoes

Clove garlic, squashed with the flat blade of a knife

Basil, torn

125g of pasta

HOW TO MAKE IT

Pierce the tomatoes with a knife and gently squeeze out the seeds over the sink. Roughly chop the tomatoes and put in a bowl with the garlic, basil leaves and a large serving spoon of olive oil. Season. If possible leave to marinate so that the flavours can develop.

Cook the pasta and just prior to draining add a spoonful of the oily salty water to the tomatoes. Remove the garlic clove. Put the drained pasta back in the saucepan and stir in the tomato sauce and serve.

PASTA GENOVESE

This is such an unlikely concoction but it is so good. Linguine or penne both work well. People make a funny face when you describe this dish but a rapturous one when they eat it.

Serves: 1X   Cooking: 25 mins   Difficulty: Easy

INGREDIENTS

125g pasta

50g green beans

2 large dessertspoons pesto

A handful of warm boiled crushed potatoes

HOW TO MAKE IT

Cook the pasta and 5 minutes before it is done according to the packet instructions, add in the green beans. Retain some cooking water before you drain. Add the pasta and beans back into the pan with the potatoes and pesto and mix thoroughly. If you feel that it needs it you can loosen up the sauce with some of the cooking water. Serve with Parmesan.

AGLIO E OLIO

Just garlic and oil, though it sounds so much better in Italian than in English. But whichever language you choose, it couldn't be much easier and I hesitate to call it a recipe.

Serves: 1X

Cooking: 15 mins

Difficulty: Easy

INGREDIENTS

Garlic

Olive oil

125g of pasta

HOW TO MAKE IT

Cook pasta according to the packet instructions. In the non-stick frying pan, gently warm some olive oil and some garlic cloves flattened with the blade of a knife. If you would like a hit of spice in this add some dried chilli seeds. Discard the cloves and toss the pasta in the warm oil and eat.

CHICKEN LIVER SAUCE

Please give this a go. I know you probably wrinkled your nose as soon as you read the word 'liver' but if you like pâté it is extremely unlikely that you will not like this. Chicken livers are an incredibly cheap source of iron and as you are an impoverished student mainlining caffeine and alcohol you may well be anaemic and iron will improve your performance in every sense.

 Serves: 1X

 Cooking: 30 mins

Difficulty: Easy

INGREDIENTS

125g chicken livers sliced into small slivers

2 dsp olive oil

1 very finely sliced small onion

Grating of nutmeg

3 dsp brandy or sherry

2 dsp tomato purée stirred into 50ml hot chicken stock (use part of a cube)

125g linguine

Parmesan

HOW TO MAKE IT

First prepare the livers. Be quite ruthless and cut away any green bile ducts or other white connective tissue. You will probably end up cutting away about 20 per cent, leaving you with approximately 100g livers.

Bring a large saucepan of water close to boiling point. In another pan very gently fry the onion in the oil for 5 minutes. Crank up the heat on the water and put the pasta in with a glug of olive oil and a large dose of salt. Add the livers to the onion and fry for a further 5 minutes. Add the alcohol if you have it and allow it to evaporate, grate over the nutmeg and add the tomato/chicken stock liquid. Cook for a few more minutes to allow the sauce to thicken. Add a large spoonful or two of salty oily pasta water to the sauce and season with pepper to taste.

By now your pasta should be al dente, drain and combine with the sauce in the frying pan and serve with plenty of grated Parmesan.

CHICKEN

KNOW

HOW

CHICKEN KNOW HOW

Without wishing to seem cynical, principles are much easier to have when you can afford them. And without wishing to sound hopelessly idealistic, if you can't hold onto principles when times are tough, then they evidently ain't your principles.

Students have long been at the vanguard of political, social and economic movements and have a noble history of protest. I remember the excitement when there was a march planned, not only on the part of the protesters, but also those planning to use the event for free travel. Generally my memory is of a student society that had ideals and ethics, obstinate in refusing to acknowledge any shades of grey and armed with the courage of its convictions.

You only need to scratch the surface of a 'how to feed the world' debate to realise what a political issue food is. Some people just don't enjoy eating meat but for many being Vegan or Vegetarian is a mission statement of their desire for farming land to become arable and thus reduce global carbon emissions (cows fart A LOT). And those vegetables are not immune from controversy either. The arguments at the core of the organic farming movement versus those who believe that world starvation can only be prevented through the cultivation of genetically modified organisms are so vicious because both sides passionately believe that the future of the human race on this Earth is at stake. Climate change, ecological balance, animal welfare, habitat loss, colony collapse, species extinction, fair-trade, food miles, all loaded, food-related phrases.

So when you amble/cycle/drive/order a delivery to your farmers' market/butcher's/supermarket to pick up your frozen/fresh/free-range/factory-farmed/ UK-raised/imported chicken you have already made a number a decisions and none of them is benign. To thine own self be true, but as you are in the midst of one of the great learning processes of your life you might as well make sure thyself has been well informed before making purchasing decisions. Saying that, you need to do so with a great deal of awareness because it seems incredibly hard to find 'pure' information that is produced with no grinding axe alongside.

I have read, looked, listened, watched and tasted and find myself firmly in the free-range/organic/humanely reared bird camp.
Personally I would rather eat less chicken than a non free-range bird. Whatever you have decided the cheapest way to buy chicken is to purchase a whole bird. Be very careful when you buy frozen chicken as it may well appear to be cheaper per kilo of frozen weight, but not necessarily defrosted weight. Often frozen poultry has emanated from the Far East where it has been reared in fairly miserable conditions. Read the label carefully as it is not unknown for food to have water added to increase weight (but that must be stated on the label).

Given that the most economical way to buy chicken is to purchase a whole bird you should know how to joint one.

The parts of a chicken can be divided into breasts, wings and legs, the latter composed of thigh and drumstick. In terms of price, high to low, the order is breast, thigh, drumstick then wing. In terms of flavour you can pretty much reverse the list. It is a complete mystery to me as to why chicken breasts are so prized in comparison to thighs because the innate taste of breast is so bland in comparison to everything else on the bird. I think that it is possibly down to squeamishness, snobbery and appearance - there is something sanitised about the white breast in comparison to the brown leg and wing joints. Whatever the reason rejoice that the bits that cost the least taste the best.

HOW TO JOINT A CHICKEN

It is of course entirely possible to buy chicken already cut into separate joints, but if you have a sharp knife it is a simple thing to do yourself. Knowledge of the bird's anatomy will also be a huge help when it comes time to carve a whole roasted bird.

Place a whole chicken on a chopping board and **make sure that your knife is sharp.** Stabilise the board with a damp tea towel underneath it. Have the wings closest to you. **Feel along the bone that runs the length of the chicken** - the breastbone. Now use your knife to cut along that bone and ease the breast away from the carcass. Keep cutting the flesh away from the bone until the breast has been detached from the bone but is still attached to the chicken via the skin. Cut the skin in such a way that the breast meat is still covered by skin. At the base of the breast where it meets the leg make a sharp lateral cut. You have now jointed your first chicken breast! Do the same with the other side. The wing will still be attached to the breast. Feel where the end of the wing bone meets the breast and cut through to separate one from the other.

Ease the thigh and drumstick away from the body of the chicken. If you turn the carcass upside down you can feel along the underside where the thigh attaches to the mid line and find an extra lump of meat called the oyster. When you cut along the line try and include the oyster with the thigh. Repeat on the other side.

Feel the point where the drumstick attaches to the thigh and locate the place in the joint where there is cartilage rather than bone - it will have more give. If you can't locate that point you can break the joint in your hands. It will give at the appropriate place and will be easier to cut through to separate the thigh from the drumstick.

You should now have 8 pieces of chicken.

Examine the chicken carcass. Ideally there should be very little flesh left on the bones but if it is your first go there is likely to be a fair amount. Practice will make perfect eventually. If you have a friendly butcher it might be an idea to buy a chicken from him/her and ask to watch how it is done by a professional.

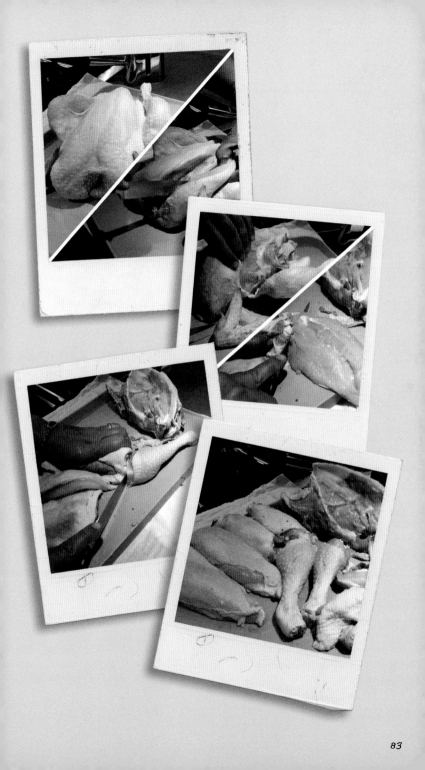

CHICKEN TRAY BAKE WITH VEGETABLES

I love this dish - there is something about it which aspires to be grown up but isn't quite there yet - it has a simplicity and innocence. If you are pushed for time it is by far the quickest way of achieving a Sunday lunch taste with little of the palaver. The only downside is that you will have to cobble together some gravy because the cooking method doesn't produce any cooking juices with which to make some.

 Serves: 1X

 Cooking: 50 mins

Difficulty: Easy

INGREDIENTS

2 chicken joints, thighs or drumsticks per person

1 large potato per person

2 each of carrots and parsnips per person

500ml chicken stock

HOW TO MAKE IT

Pre-heat the oven to 180°C. Peel the vegetables and chop them into 2.5cm sized pieces. Par boil them until they are partially cooked.

Use the saucepan lid to drain the cooking liquid into a small saucepan into which you have placed a chicken stock cube. Place a roasting tray in the oven with a splash of cooking oil. After 5 minutes remove the tray and tip in the vegetables.

Roast for 20 minutes and then carefully, using a fish slice to prise them off so as not to lose the crispy crust, turn the vegetables.

Add in the chicken pieces (skin side down if using thighs) and pour on 100ml of the stock. Season and return to the oven. Turn again in 20 minutes.

In the meantime, add a teaspoon of Marmite to the remaining chicken stock. Make a mixture of two teaspoons of cornflour and two teaspoons of water. Stir this into the stock and then gently heat, stirring all the while unless you like lumpy gravy. Taste and adjust the seasoning if necessary.

Remove the chicken pieces from the oven and leave to rest underneath a piece of foil and return the vegetables to the oven for a final blast, cranking the oven up a notch or two if they seem to be insufficiently roasted.

Serve with a green leafy vegetable.

CHEAT'S BARBECUE CHICKEN

You can of course buy barbecue sauce off the shelf and there are some pretty good ones out there, but this is a quick cheap version that will do nicely.

Serves: 4

Cooking: 45 mins

Difficulty: Easy

INGREDIENTS

12 wings, 8 thighs or 8 drumsticks

100ml ketchup

2 large dsp of runny honey

3 dsp Worcestershire sauce

3 dsp soy sauce

1 dsp marmalade

1 tsp chilli flakes

HOW TO MAKE IT

Put all the ingredients in a large dish and stir until thoroughly mixed. Check the seasoning and then coat the chicken pieces in the sauce. Bake in an oven pre-heated to 180°C.

Cook for 30 to 40 minutes, turning the chicken joints every 10 minutes or so and basting them with the sauce at the same time.

CHICKEN WITH CHILLI, MINT AND GARLIC

A quick and simple dish, but tasty and satisfyingly sticky.

Serves: 4

Cooking: 50 mins

Difficulty: Easy

INGREDIENTS

12 wings, 8 thighs or 8 drumsticks

2 dsp honey

Juice of an orange

1 tsp dried chilli flakes

2 crushed cloves of garlic

A handful of fresh finely chopped mint

HOW TO MAKE IT

In a bowl, mix together the honey, chilli, orange juice and garlic. Toss the chicken wings in the mixture and add in some finely chopped mint. Cook in an oven pre-heated to 180°C for 45 minutes, turning every 15 minutes or so.

Serve with rice or a salad.

THIGHS WITH THYME HONEY & GARLIC

This could easily be done with wings or drumsticks too.

Serves: 2X

Cooking: 45 mins

Difficulty: Easy

INGREDIENTS

4 chicken thighs

2 dsp honey

Handful of thyme leaves

Juice of a lemon

2 cloves of crushed garlic

HOW TO MAKE IT

Mix the honey, thyme leaves and garlic together with the juice of a lemon. Toss in the thighs and then bake at 180°C for 40 minutes, turning over half way.

HERB GRILLED CHICKEN

Breasts work well for this dish but thigh fillets not only taste better, but also cost a lot less. This chicken is fantastic tossed into a salad or eaten in a wrap with lettuce, bacon, avocado, Parmesan, tomato - whatever takes your fancy.

Serves 2

Marinating: 30 mins
Cooking: 30 mins

Difficulty: Easy

INGREDIENTS

6 thigh fillets or 2 breasts
1 dsp dried oregano
2 cloves crushed garlic
Juice of a lemon

HOW TO MAKE IT

Mix the lemon juice with a splash of olive oil, the garlic and oregano and pour over the chicken. Leave to marinate for 30 minutes before grilling the chicken on foil. After about 8 minutes on each side for thighs (15 minutes on each side for breasts) check that the chicken feels firm to the touch. Double check that the juices run clear when a fork/skewer is stuck into the thickest part of the meat. If it is cooked through, turn off the grill and wrap the chicken in the foil to rest for at least ten minutes.

ROAST
CHICKEN

HOW TO ROAST A CHICKEN

There are many benefits to leaving home - the exercise of free will, the voyage of discovery that living in a new place can take you on, the absence of nagging, interfering, eyebrow raising judgemental parents. Freedom. Amongst the downsides is the fact that the only way to put Sunday lunch on your table is to cook it yourself. I am starting you off with a roast chicken because it is the least exacting to cook, the most forgiving of a dodgy oven, the easiest to carve and the most useful as a leftover. I am going to take you through the timings of getting chicken, gravy, roasties and your other veg on the table at the same time because this seems to be quite daunting at first.

There are dozens of ways that you can prepare a chicken for roasting, this just happens to be my favourite.

Serves: 4-6   Cooking: 2 hours   Difficulty: Easy

INGREDIENTS

30g very soft butter

Lemon

One fat clove of garlic smashed in its skin

1.8kg chicken

Herbs - rosemary, sage, thyme

400ml chicken stock from a cube

HOW TO MAKE IT

Oven pre-heated to 200°C.

Put the chicken into the roasting dish - hopefully it will be quite snug. Squeeze the juice of the lemon over the bird and place the halves of lemon inside the convenient cavity - this is situated at the opposite end of the chicken to where the wings are. Add the herbs and the squashed garlic to the cavity. Smear the skin of the chicken with the butter, sprinkle some salt over that then add the chicken stock to the roasting dish. Put in the oven and turn the heat down after twenty minutes to 180°C.

After a further one hours and ten minutes remove the chicken from the oven and test for doneness by inserting a skewer into the meatiest part of the leg. If the juices run out clear the chicken is cooked. If there is still a trace of pink in the juices return the chicken to the oven for another 10 minutes and then test again.

The clear juices test is the standard one for chicken. My favourite test though for a whole roast chicken is this one. Take a piece of kitchen roll and fold it until it is the size of a standard post-it note. Use that to protect your fingers whilst grasping the end of the drumstick. If you can twist the drumstick bone and pull it out of the chicken it is done. If you meet with resistance then the bird needs to be cooked for a bit longer. The beauty of the drumstick removal test is that you have just made the job of carving that much easier.

If your bird is cooked leave it to rest on a carving board covered in foil for about 15 minutes or longer if that suits you. Resting allows the juices to relax back into the bird and will make the chicken more juicy and tender than if you eat it straight out of the oven.

Whilst the bird is resting spoon the fat off from the juices that have collected in the roasting dish. The fat will be a clear substance that rises above the rest of the liquid. Spoon the fat into something like a used yoghurt pot.

Once the fat is cool chill in the fridge and then spoon into your food waste. That way it will get recycled and will not clog up your drains. Taste the now de-fatted juices and season. You may want to concentrate them by boiling them up briefly in a saucepan or they may taste just right already, in which case spoon them over the chicken when you are ready to serve.

Really the simplest way to divide up the chicken is to joint the thigh, wing and drumstick as described on p.82. Then carve downwards through the breast to produce elegant slices.

SUNDAY ROAST

If you want to do the full monty Sunday lunch here is your timetable, 'T' being the time at which you would like to eat.

T-2 hours 50 minutes
Remove the chicken from the fridge.

T-2 hours
Pre-heat the oven to 200°C. Make sure that the oven shelves are set in the right place to take the chicken and a tray of roasties.

Prepare the chicken as described on p.96.

Peel potatoes and parsnips. Cut the parsnips into 3...a long triangle shape, and the thick end bit cut into two lengthways. The potatoes should be cut into evenly sized shapes, a little larger than a golf ball.

Par boil the parsnips and potatoes so that they are partially cooked - they should give a little when you put a knife into them. Drain off the water and keep it in a bowl/jug for making gravy later. Put the saucepan lid back on the potatoes/parsnips.

Peel the carrots and cut into batons by cutting the carrot lengthways in half (and half again if it is particularly large) and then cut across the carrot to make 5cm lengths. Put the carrots in a saucepan with a knob of butter and a splash of water.

T-1 hour 50 minutes
Put the chicken in the oven. Also put in the oven a roasting dish with a thin layer of some type of fat - sunflower oil, light olive oil, beef dripping, lard, duck fat - the choice is varied and yours. Just don't use a strongly flavoured oil or an extra virgin olive oil.

T-1 hour 30 minutes
Turn the oven down to 180°C

T- 1 hour 15
Check that there is no water left in the potato/parsnip saucepan. With the lid on jiggle them about so that the edges are roughed up a bit. Remove the pan with oil from the oven and carefully put the potatoes and parsnips in. They should sizzle. Sprinkle them with salt and put the tray into the oven as quickly as possible to minimise heat loss.

Turn to page 100.

T-45 minutes

Check the potatoes and parsnips, carefully turning them over and moving them around the pan to ensure that they are all cooking evenly.

T-20 minutes

Remove the chicken from the oven and test for doneness by using the drumstick test. If it is cooked, cover the chicken with foil to keep warm, otherwise return it to the oven for another 10 minutes.

Check the potatoes and parsnips. They should be browning nicely. Using a rigid spatula, turn them over carefully so as not to leave the crusty bit on the pan but keep it attached to the potato where it belongs. If they still seem a bit underwhelming, crank the oven back to 200°C when you return them there.

Put the carrots on a medium heat on the hob. Keep the lid on them so that they partially steam. They may need a splash more water. Once they are cooked to your liking, add a handful of frozen petits pois, put the lid back on and turn off the heat.

Remove the chicken to a carving board. If there is any fat in the roasting pan, spoon it off into a bowl until there is only one dessertspoon remaining. In a cup put a few dessertspoons of the chicken juices together with 2 dessertspoons of plain flour and mix well so that there are no lumps. Put the roasting dish on a low heat on the hob. Add the flour mixture and a teaspoon of Marmite to the pan. Use a fork at this stage to ease any tasty gooey bits of roast chicken residue off the bottom of the pan and ensure that no lumps are forming. The gravy should start to bubble and thicken. Taste it. If it is too strong or thick add some of the parsnip water, if it needs to be saltier add a bit more Marmite. Once you are happy with it, put it on a back burner.

T-10 minutes

Check the potatoes. If they look as if they are nearly good to go then you can start getting your ducks in a line. Warm the plates in the oven for 5 minutes. Reheat the carrots and peas, check the temperature of the gravy and start carving the chicken. Remove the potatoes and parsnips from the oven, plate it all up and enjoy!

ROAST CHICKEN WITH PEPPERS

This is a firm favourite in my family - it is very colourful and somewhat lighter than the traditional roast potato/parsnip accompaniments. It also produces great leftovers for a ciabatta sandwich.

Serves: 4

Cooking: 2 hours

Difficulty: Easy

INGREDIENTS

Peppers, red, orange or yellow (2 or 3 per person)

Bulb of garlic

1.8kg chicken

500ml chicken stock

HOW TO MAKE IT

In a small saucepan, boil the whole bulb of garlic for 20 minutes. Slice the peppers through in half lengthways and remove the stem, core and seeds. Peppers helpfully show you convenient places to slice through them so make life easy and go along with their suggestions. You should have 6 to 8 long strips per pepper.

Place the peppers at the base of a roasting dish and scatter the garlic cloves over the peppers. Place the chicken on top, pour over some olive oil, season and roast at 200°C for 20 minutes then pour in the chicken stock and roast for a further hour at 180°C. Remove the chicken to rest, pour off the juices into a saucepan and return the peppers and garlic to the oven whilst the chicken rests. Turn up the oven to 200°C if the peppers appear under-roasted.

Spoon off any oil from the juices and season to taste. Serve with bread.

LEFTOVER CHICKEN

The great thing about mastering the roast chicken is that you will hopefully have leftovers and therefore a large number of meal options. I suggest that you leave the chicken on the bone and well wrapped in the fridge to keep it moist.

Sandwiches are the easiest and most obvious choice - taking a wrap to the library will be far cheaper and taste better than buying one from a shop.

Bacon, lettuce, tomatoes, avocado, peppers and watercress are all great partners with chicken.

You can make a quick curried chicken sandwich with a mixture of mayo, mango chutney and a teaspoon of curry powder.

A chicken **salad** is a delicious supper especially when combined with the aforementioned bacon and avocado.

The **risotto** in the Veggie-ish section is good with a handful of chicken and it is a great addition to a soup.

CHICKEN BROTH

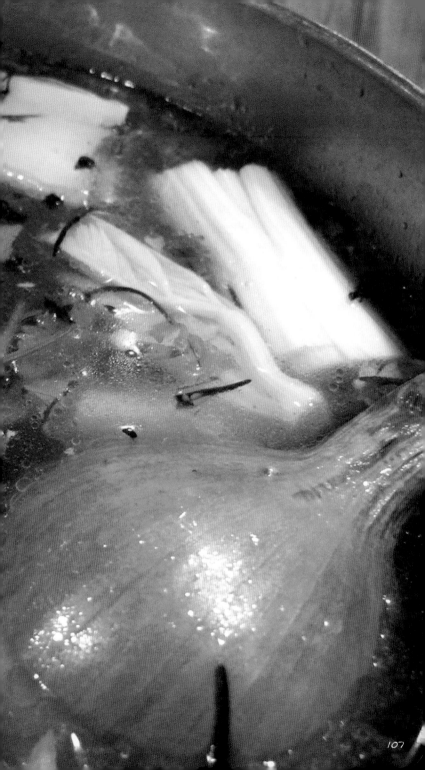

CHICKEN BROTH

To be honest, it would never have occurred to me to include this recipe had the boys with whom I tested some of the recipes in this book not asked. Broth is a fantastic heartwarming bowl of goodness that is made from things that normally end up in the bin. It doesn't take a lot of effort to make and that effort is amply rewarded by the taste of the result. It's a win win. Without wishing to sound bonkers, I believe in the healing powers of chicken broth and when you have tasted the good stuff, so shall you too.

Makes 1 litre   Cooking: 1 hour   Difficulty: Easy

INGREDIENTS

A whole unpeeled onion

A scrubbed carrot or two

Maybe a cleaned leek, the white part

A couple of ribs of celery, especially the leafy ones

A few stems of parsley

Several whole peppercorns

A bay leaf

A tomato

A chicken carcass

HOW TO MAKE IT

Keep the remains of the roasted chicken in the dish in which it was roasted. Scrape any of the jellied juices that escaped from the bird whilst it was resting back into the roasting dish. When you have a couple of hours in which you are going to be near your stove to keep an eye on your simmering stock, put the following into a large clean pan:

The contents of the roasting dish, chicken carcass torn roughly apart, juices et al but minus the lemon and spent herbs that may have been in the cavity.

Cover that lot plus the remaining ingredients with water, bring it to the boil and then allow to simmer away for a couple of hours with the lid on but slightly ajar.

Once it has cooled down a bit, strain the stock into a clean bowl. As soon at the stock is cool enough to do so, refrigerate it.

A layer of fat will solidify on the surface and it will be easy to skim off once it is solid. If you are in need of chicken stock in the following days then, hey presto, you have an additive-free wholesome supply. It is brilliant for a risotto but also amazing for chicken noodle soup, which is easy enough to make by adding - you guessed it - chicken and noodles.

Other nice additions are some diced carrot or celery and mint leaves added just before eating are particularly uplifting. Or you can turn it into more of an Asian thing by adding lemongrass, shredded lime leaves, a chopped red chilli and a good squeeze of a lime and some mint leaves.

If you do not have an immediate use for it and would like to freeze it but have limited space, you can concentrate the stock by reducing its volume by boiling it. It is brilliant for making gravy and if you have a particularly fine batch, try cooking pasta in it - it will be the most delicious pasta you will ever have tasted.

GROUND

MEAT

GROUND MEAT

I really don't like the word 'mince'. And as this is my book and I get to choose, I choose 'ground'.

Typically whole pieces of meat cost more per kilo because ground meat often contains some fairly random pieces of an animal.

There is a long and delicious list of things that can be made with ground meat - burgers, stuffings, meat balls, shepherd's pie, Bolognese sauce and because it is accessible in terms of ease of availability as well as price, this chapter has a number of ideas for you to play with.

BURGERS AND MEATBALLS

Burgers

It is entirely possible to buy some ground meat, season it, form it into a ball shape then flatten it, grill it and hey presto you have a burger. Easy peasy. Add a burger bun and ketchup and you have a classic. But you can also have fun playing around with various seasonings and pairings to spice up your life with some variety. If you find that they are falling apart try adding an egg before you form them into burgers. To cook them, pre-heat the grill and then place the burgers on foil. Once they have browned to your satisfaction on one side, turn them over. It is particularly important that pork and turkey burgers are cooked through before eating and it will help if the patties are on the small side. Leave them to rest for 5 minutes before serving.

Beef

The range of ground beef available stretches from ground steak (usually sirloin) down to ground chuck. The range of fat content can go from 7% to about 50%. Somewhere in the middle is probably where you want a burger if you are aiming for juicy rather than dry. 180g is a decent serving, approximately a tennis ball size before it is flattened. If you want to make something a little bit more economical, season the meat, add some grated raw onion and sometimes some finely chopped parsley or chives. Occasionally I add some Worcestershire sauce to the mix. For a change from chips, as an accompaniment, cut sweet potato into thin chip-like shapes, toss in a small amount of olive oil and a pinch of paprika and bake on parchment for 30 minutes at 180°C, turning halfway.

BURGERS AND MEATBALLS (CONTINUED)

Lamb
Lamb is a fairly fat laden meat and personally I find it too fatty for burgers - at least when you make moussaka or shepherd's pie you can spoon the fat off. Grilling obviously helps to drain some of the fat away and seasonings that work well with lamb include mint, chilli and garlic. Serve the burgers in pittas with Cos lettuce leaves and some mint or chilli jelly.

Pork
Counter intuitively ground pork is fairly lean and can be dry. You can make some impressive Asian style burgers or dumplings for soup with pork. Ground pork is also an essential for making stuffing. Of course the most widely available form of (very) ground pork is the immensely popular banger. To some coarsely ground pork you can add coriander, lemon grass, finely chopped lime leaves. Make sure the patties are on the small size so that they can cook through. Also they have a tendency to dry out on the grill, so try frying them in a small amount of oil in a non-stick pan.

Turkey
You can make some cracking meatballs and burgers with ground turkey - just try and find ground turkey thigh rather than breast as it is cheaper and has more flavour. Turkey is high in protein and low in fat, so if you are not careful, turkey burgers can be as dry as old boots. I usually rectify this by adding some cold finely chopped onion that I have turned to a nice golden brown with some olive oil in a frying pan. Coriander and chives work very well with these but as turkey is so bland, it will absorb virtually any flavour or spice that you throw at it.

Chicken
The least flavoursome and most expensive option, as it is difficult to find anything other than ground chicken breast. And ground chicken just seems incredibly sticky. Avoid I say.

CHILLI CON CARNE

I developed a strong aversion to chilli con carne as in my catering days I made seemingly endless amounts of this. Now on the evening that I help cook at a homeless shelter this is what is on the menu, so it seems that there is no escape! But it is easy, versatile and a real crowd pleaser. I am never sure about freezing it with the kidney beans, as I once had an exploding bean issue that was very smelly and unpleasant. But I think that was just my bad luck, as I have never heard of anyone else having this problem. Most proper chilli con carne is made with cubed rather than ground beef but the latter has become ubiquitous.

Serves: 4-6

Cooking: 1¼ hours

Difficulty: Easy

INGREDIENTS

900g - 1kg ground beef

800g tin chopped tomatoes

2 onions finely chopped

1 tsp each of cumin, chilli powder, smoked paprika

½ tsp cinnamon and/or allspice

1 tsp each of salt and sugar

400g tin kidney beans, drained and well rinsed.

HOW TO MAKE IT

Cook the onion in 2 dessertspoons of flavourless oil until it is soft but not coloured. Add in the spices and stir thoroughly. Remove the onion from the pan, turn up the heat and brown the meat to seal it, stirring all the time. Add back the onion, stir thoroughly, then add the tomatoes, sugar and salt. Turn down the heat and allow to simmer away for 45 minutes or so, stirring occasionally.

Add the kidney beans and adjust the seasoning. If it is not hot enough for your liking add some chopped fresh red chillies.

This is great served on its own with guacamole, sour cream, lettuce and tortilla shells, with rice or a jacket potato. It is definitely one of those meals that taste even better a couple of days after it has been made and a very handy thing to have in the freezer to warm you up on a grey winter's day.

LIGHTER SHEPHERDS PIE

I was once making shepherd's pie without really giving it my full attention and at least doubled the amount of carrot that I normally put in. I have to say I preferred it and if you are trying to eat less meat and more vegetables then this is one way forward - plus it is more economical as carrots are a great deal cheaper than lamb.

Serves: 4

Cooking: 1¼ hours

Difficulty: Easy

INGREDIENTS

2 onions finely chopped

500g ground lamb

1 dsp dried mint

3 large, finely grated carrots

Worcestershire sauce

Ketchup

Tomato puree

HOW TO MAKE IT

Dry fry the onions in a non-stick pan with the mint by turning them frequently so that the onions do not burn and then remove them from the pan so that you can start sealing the ground lamb, turning it over as it browns.

Lamb is an incredibly fatty meat which is why it is best not to add any extra oil if you can possibly avoid it. Add the carrot and the onion to the lamb with a large glug of Worcestershire sauce and a similarly liberal dose of tomato ketchup, as well as a good squeeze of a tube of tomato puree.

Taste as you go along so that you can adjust it to your liking. It is likely to need a large spoonful of salt. When it tastes good and it has simmered away for half an hour or so, leave it to cool.

The fat will rise to the surface so spoon it off into a container so that you can discard it later.

Transfer the meat into a baking dish. Boil sufficient potatoes to cover the top of whatever dish that you are using.

One large jacket sized potato per person is probably about the right amount. If you don't have a potato masher, baking the potatoes and then scooping out the insides with a fork will work well.

Bake for 20 minutes at 180°C. This will freeze beautifully but I would freeze it without the potato, as it absorbs lots of water when frozen and tends to go a bit sludgy.

TOAD IN THE HOLE

This is a ridiculously delicious treat. The recipe I use is almost entirely
Nigel Slater's from his Real Food book with some tweaked quantities.

Serves: 1X   Cooking: 45 mins   Difficulty: Easy

INGREDIENTS

1 egg

4 heaped dsp plain flour

75ml milk mixed with
75ml water

1 dsp grain mustard

2 sausages, in half

4 rashers of pancetta
(the type that looks like
streaky bacon, not the
cubed kind)

HOW TO MAKE IT

Pre-heat the oven to 220°C. Mix the eggs, flour,
milk and mustard with some salt and pepper,
whisking with a fork until all the lumps of flour
have disappeared and leave to stand for 15
minutes or so.

Put a small oven-proof dish in the oven with a
couple of dessertspoons of oil. De-skin and half
the sausages and wrap each one in a piece of
pancetta.

Remove the dish from the oven, put in the
sausages, and then pour on the batter. Bake for
25–30 minutes till golden.

Serve with a leafy green vegetable to help redress
the health balance.

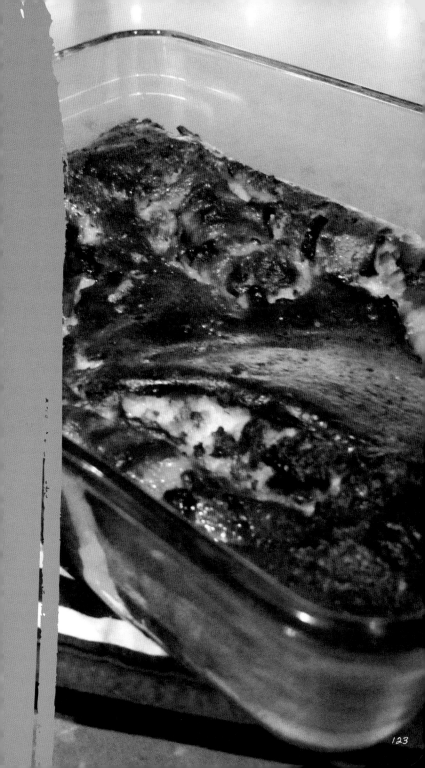

SAUSAGE AND LENTIL CASSEROLE

This tastes even better a few days after it has been made, so it is worth making more than you need. And don't leave out the bay leaves. They don't make a huge amount of difference to the taste but they are a natural anti-flatulent so probably wiser to keep them in.

Serves: 2X

Cooking: 1 hour

Difficulty: Easy

INGREDIENTS

70g cubed pancetta or 4 rashers of smoked, streaky bacon

Bay leaves

6 pork sausages

2 red onions, cut in half and then sliced into semi circles

4 finely chopped tomatoes

6 large palmfuls of green lentils

500ml chicken stock made up with a stock cube

HOW TO MAKE IT

Sauté the onion in a glug of oil until it collapses and is starting to brown. Add in the pancetta, turning until it is cooked through and then remove the onion and pancetta, leaving behind as much oil as possible by tipping the pan. Brown the sausages. If there is a great deal of fat in the pan, drain it off, leaving a dessertspoon remaining. Stir in the lentils, bay leaves and tomatoes then add back the onions and pancetta. When it is all thoroughly mixed, add in the stock. Bring to the boil and them simmer for half an hour by which time the sausages will be soft and cooked through. You can make this a one-pot wonder by adding in some frozen spinach cubes 10 minutes before serving. If you happen to have a tub of crème fraîche, a spoonful is a very nice addition.

The only thing about this dish that is not great is the colour. I tend to serve it with a colourful vegetable such as sweet potato. Bake whole sweet potatoes in the oven in a roasting dish for an hour at 180°C, until they are soft. When they are cool enough to handle, slice them in half and scoop out the flesh into a bowl. It should be quite mashed enough but you can use a fork if you want to mash it further.

PEPPERS STUFFED WITH THE CONTENTS OF THE FRIDGE

The genesis of this recipe came from the random ingredients in my fridge but you can of course adapt it to the contents of your cupboards. It could contain pork or turkey, or no meat at all. In the Mediterranean, peppers are often stuffed with leftover rice or couscous. Different herbs, some anchovies, some cubes of mozzarella - whatever. This is really about using a minimal amount of meat and using up lots of leftovers.

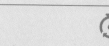

Serves: 4

Cooking: 1 hour

Difficulty: Easy

INGREDIENTS

2 finely chopped onions

A large handful of baby plum tomatoes

3 cloves garlic

1 dsp finely chopped rosemary

A handful of shredded baby spinach leaves

Zest of a lemon

250g ground beef

1 rasher of bacon, chopped

A few mushrooms, finely chopped

4 red peppers, halved through the stalk and deseeded, stalks left intact

A handful of breadcrumbs

HOW TO MAKE IT

Pre-heat the oven to 180°C.

In a pan of boiling water, cook the pepper halves for 5 minutes. Remove to a baking tray, skin side down.

Sweat the onion in olive oil until soft but not coloured. Add the rosemary, garlic and tomatoes until they collapse. Remove this to a bowl.

In the same pan, cook the bacon, then add the beef and brown lightly and add the mushrooms. Combine this with the onion-garlic-tomato mush, grate in the lemon zest and season to taste. Spoon the mixture into the pepper halves, drizzle over some olive oil and sprinkle some breadcrumbs on top and bake for 30 minutes at 180°C until the stuffing is piping hot. Serve with a green salad or vegetables.

MEATBALLS

I really love meatballs. Small little bursts of flavour, it is hard to think of a culture that does not have its own version. This really is an opportunity to use your imagination.

To any type of ground meat you can add finely chopped onions, herbs, spices, seasonings, breadcrumbs. Here are just a few suggestions but there are no hard and fast rules other than finely chopped applies across the board:

Beef, breadcrumbs, Worcestershire sauce, onion.

Pork, soy sauce, spring onion, lime leaf, lemon grass.

Lamb, garlic, ginger, cumin, mint, garam masala, coriander.

As for cooking, there are options a plenty. They can be browned in a small amount of oil until they are cooked through completely or they can be simmered in stock once they have been browned or finished in the oven.

Nigella Lawson has a completely brilliant method of dropping tiny little balls of ground pork, beef and finely chopped onion into bubbling tomato sauce to cook them through and the Vietnamese style pork balls lend themselves to being cooked through in a broth and served with noodles.

MIDDLE EASTERN TURKEY MEATBALLS

This is a recipe that I have adapted from Yotam Ottolenghi and Sami Tamimi's book 'Jerusalem'. They freeze well and are delicious with pitta and hummus or with rice.

Approx: 9 meatballs

Cooking: 1 hour

Difficulty: Easy

INGREDIENTS

500g ground turkey (thighs rather than breast if possible)

1 large grated courgette

1 egg

1 bunch finely sliced spring onions

2 dsp each of chopped mint and coriander

2 crushed garlic cloves

1 tsp each of ground cumin and salt

½ tsp each of cayenne and black pepper

50ml sunflower oil

HOW TO MAKE IT

Line an oven tray with greaseproof paper and pre-heat the oven to 200°C. Pour a thin layer of oil into your non-stick frying pan and place on the hob.

Mix together all the ingredients except the oil. Take a dessertspoon of the mixture and form into a rugby ball type shape by rolling the mixture in your hands. At this stage you can freeze the balls on a baking sheet in the freezer.

After about 8 hours, ease them off the sheet and into a plastic freezer bag, excluding as much air as possible. If cooking immediately, turn on the heat and when the oil is hot, put the meatballs into the oil and brown them in batches, adding more oil if necessary.

Once they are brown, transfer to the oven tray and heat through in the oven for 10 minutes.

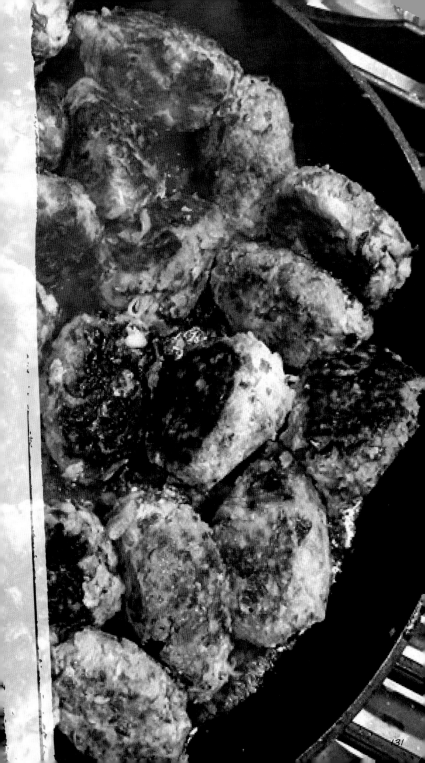

DON'T
TAKE IT
AWAY...

DON'T TAKE IT AWAY, DO IT YOURSELF

Student life is full of contradictions. On the one hand you are undergoing the most immersive learning experience since you took on walking and talking so your intellectual capabilities are immense but on the other you are hell bent on leaving no club, bar or pub undiscovered. The chances are that you are abusing your young and fit body with alcohol and when suitably inebriated you will turn to a take away to soak up some alcohol - hello kebab/chip/pizza van.

Because owing to the lack of discernment amongst its invariably incoherent customer base, your average take-away in your average university town will aim at the lowest common denominator. That is you by the way. And if you don't believe me, go and eat from one when you are sober.

The fact that you have even read this far means that there is hope for you. I bear the great tidings that if you can be arsed to make the following dishes at home they will taste a great deal better and cost a great deal less than from your local take-away. You will miss out on the repetitive onion breath the next morning but that is just the sacrifice that you will have to make.

Just a word of warning - the safest thing to make when you get home rather the worse for wear is a bowl of cereal. Next up is toast. DO NOT do what my husband used to do as a student, which is try to grill dodgy oil-covered frozen spring rolls from Brick Lane and set fire to the kitchen.

KEEMA

I always think of this spicy comfort food as Indian shepherd's pie - my father always seemed to have a bowl of this in his fridge.

Serves: 3X

Cooking: 1 hour

Difficulty: Easy

INGREDIENTS

2 onions peeled and chopped

1 dsp each of ground coriander and cumin

1 tsp each of ground ginger, garam masala and turmeric

2 red chillis seeds in or out, depending on how hot you like things

1 large man's thumb of ginger, grated

2 cloves garlic, grated

½ tsp cayenne

450g ground lamb

340g tin chopped tomatoes

HOW TO MAKE IT

Heat the onions in a small amount of flavourless oil in your non-stick wok and cook until very soft and slightly coloured.

Add in all the spices and give a good stir. Push the contents of the pan to one side and add the lamb and brown whilst breaking up with your spoon so that the pieces stay small.

Once all the meat has browned, amalgamate it with the rest of the wok contents and taste. If it is not right, adjust the seasoning - more cumin will add warmth, coriander heat and cayenne even more heat. Season with salt too, lamb seems to need quite a bit.

Add the tin of tomatoes and cook at a brisk simmer for 30 to 40 minutes. Keep tasting - it might even need a small amount of sugar if it is too acidic.

Once cooked, turn the heat off and make a well in the meat on one of the edges of the pan. Leave for 5 to 10 minutes and then spoon off the fat that will have gathered.

To this mixture can be added a number of vegetables. A diced rinsed potato can go in at the same time as the tomatoes, or fresh or frozen leaf spinach can be added towards the end - aubergine too would work, though this would be best added to the pan after the onion and coloured prior to adding the lamb.

Peas are probably the most ubiquitous addition, but in a country as large as India it is hard to generalise. Quite often the mixture is used to stuff a Naan bread.

This freezes very well, though it is best to freeze it without the vegetables

NOT QUITE TANDOORI CHICKEN OR LAMB

The Tandoori mixture that I use is from 'Seasoned Pioneers' but I expect that you will find it hard to track down. Bizarrely, most supermarkets sell every type of Indian rub, sauce or paste except this one. I wouldn't accuse my version of being very authentic but it is nonetheless delicious and unlike more sauce-laden curries, this one is not overly filling. It is very nice served with naan bread, a chutney and some cucumber raita made from mixing diced cucumber, natural yoghurt and mint.

Serves: 2X

Marinating: Overnight
Cooking: 45 mins

Difficulty: Easy

INGREDIENTS

450g filleted chicken thighs or lamb neck fillets

4 cloves grated garlic

Little finger of grated ginger

1 dsp Tandoori spice mixture or 1 dsp garam masala

1 tsp turmeric

½ tsp chilli powder

Juice of a lemon

3 dsp natural yoghurt

HOW TO MAKE IT

Mix together all the ingredients except the yoghurt and rub into the chicken or lamb. After half an hour, add the yoghurt and leave overnight. Freeze whatever you don't need for later use.

Pre-heat the grill and when it is hot, cook the chicken for 10 minutes on each side, the lamb fillets will take about 15 on each side.

They should be slightly charred. Wrap in the foil and leave to rest for 10 minutes or so before serving.

THAI CHICKEN AND AUBERGINE CURRY

THAI CHICKEN AND AUBERGINE CURRY

If you are fortunate enough to live near a Thai shop, I would advise you to buy ingredients for this recipe there. They are likely to be much cheaper than in a supermarket and in addition they may sell fresh ready-made curry pastes. My local Thai shop sells the pastes for red, yellow and green curries as well as Jungle, Malay and Panang. They are very good and are definitely easier and probably cheaper than assembling the ingredients for your own curry paste.

If, on the other hand, you don't have a Thai shop and/or are feeling adventurous, give this a go. This curry is fresh tasting and can be made without a blender. Leftovers can be stored in the fridge once cooled and reheated until piping hot for another meal. Lemongrass keeps for quite a while in the fridge and lime leaves freeze very well.

This is an adaptation of a Nigel Slater curry - so adapted that I am not sure that he would recognise it but it was definitely inspired by him. You could easily turn this into a vegetarian dish by upping the aubergine or adding mushrooms and omitting the chicken and a handful of raw prawns could easily replace the chicken.

Serves: 2X | Cooking: 45 mins | Difficulty: Medium

INGREDIENTS

1 aubergine cut into 2.5cm chunks

1 bunch spring onions cut into 2.5cm lengths

2 finely chopped garlic cloves

1 red chilli, deseeded if you don't like your curry too hot

2 lemongrass hearts finely chopped

400ml can coconut milk

2 pak choi stripped from their stems and halved lengthwise if large

6 chicken thigh fillets, approximately 400g, cut into bite sized chunks

Juice of a lime

2 dsp nam pla (fish sauce)

1 tsp sugar

1 tsp salt

8 or so very finely shredded lime leaves

1 large handful of torn sweet Thai basil leaves

HOW TO MAKE IT

Put the last six ingredients into a jar, close the lid firmly and shake. The easiest way to shred the lime leaves is to put all the leaves on top of each other and then roll them into a cylinder and slice across the cylinder as finely as you can, so you end up with tiny little ribbons of lime leaf.

Prepare all the other ingredients. It is hard to believe how many layers of unyielding lemongrass that you have to peel away to get to the soft heart but you will know when you get to it because it is very easy to cut through. Remember that chilli can burn your skin, so wash your hands and the board after cutting it and do not touch your eyes or any other delicate parts of your anatomy soon after.

Heat your non-stick wok on a medium heat and when you can feel that the pan is hot, add a few dessertspoons of flavourless oil and stir-fry the aubergine until it is coloured, then remove it to a bowl. Turn down the heat a bit and add another dessertspoon of oil and gently cook the spring onion, garlic, lemongrass and chilli until they are soft. Move these to the same bowl as the aubergine, leaving behind as much oil as possible in the pan. Turn up the heat and then stir-fry the chicken until it is coloured on the outside, then add the aubergine/onion, etc back into the pan. After 5 minutes, add the contents of the screw-top jar and stir around for a few minutes before adding the coconut milk and allow to bubble away. Taste and season if necessary. Just before serving, add the pak choi and stir for a minute so that it collapses but doesn't lose its vibrant green colour.

Serve with plain rice or noodles.

PIZZAS

I am really excited about how simple and quick these pizzas are. They are thin and tasty and take less than 5 minutes to cook in the oven. The recipe below is simply a blueprint - you know better than anyone what you like on a pizza, so go with that.

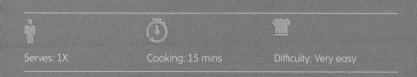

Serves: 1X

Cooking: 15 mins

Difficulty: Very easy

INGREDIENTS

A flatbread the size of a dinner plate - Italian by preference but a thickish tortilla wrap will do

1 dsp of tomato sauce or purée

A large handful of grated mozzarella

1 sausage, skinned, torn into pieces and dry fried in a non-stick pan

1 red chilli, deseeded and cut into thin strips

HOW TO MAKE IT

Heat the oven to 220°C. Smear the flatbread with tomato sauce/purée and then grate over the mozzarella.

Scatter the chilli and the sausage and then put in the oven for 5 minutes.

Serve with a salad.

LEBANESE
LAMB KEBABS

This is my boy's favourite meal. The marinade for the lamb is Middle Eastern and inspired by a recipe that I first came across in a book called 'Blistering Barbecues', though I have changed mine from the original significantly. If you have a Middle Eastern shop nearby buy the spices there - they will be much cheaper than at the supermarket.

Serves: 2X

Marinating: Overnight
Cooking: 30 mins

Difficulty: Easy

INGREDIENTS

2 lamb neck fillets

2 dsp sumac powder

4 dsp pomegranate molasses

1 dsp ground cumin

1 tsp cayenne

Peel of a lemon

6 dsp natural yoghurt

HOW TO MAKE IT

Put all the ingredients apart from the lamb into a large zip-loc bag or bowl, mix thoroughly and then put in the fillets, halved for ease of fitting and for jiggling around in the marinade.

Marinate overnight in the fridge. If you want to make a larger quantity you could freeze any excess lamb in the marinade in freezer bags. The effect of this marinade is warm and spicy rather than hot. If you want hotter, add in some more cayenne or some flaked chilli seeds.

Ideally, these should be barbecued but grilled works well too. I like lamb quite pink but this cut is better when served medium.

Pre-heat the grill and then cook each side of the fillets for about 8 minutes but obviously the timings depend on your grill and the thickness of the fillets. Leave them to rest before cutting into diagonal chunks and serving with hummus, tsatsiki, chilli jelly and lettuce leaves in flatbread.

CHICKEN SHAWARMISH

Again the Shawarma spices are from 'Seasoned Pioneers' but I think that you will find them hard to track down. If you find a spice mixture called 'Baharat' it will do nicely. This recipe should probably contain cardamom but even I couldn't be bothered to peel and crush the pods, so I doubt that you would be either.

 Serves: 2X

Marinating: Overnight
Cooking: 25 mins

 Difficulty: Easy

INGREDIENTS

450g chicken thigh fillets

3 cloves of grated garlic

1 finger of grated ginger

1 dsp shawarma/baharat spices or 1 tsp each of allspice, black pepper, cinnamon, cumin, coriander

3 dsp oil

Juice of a lemon

Lettuce

FOR THE SAUCE:

Juice of a lemon

1 tsp tahini

3 dsp natural yoghurt

¼ of a cucumber

1 tsp sumac

1 clove grated garlic

TO SERVE:

Pitta bread

HOW TO MAKE IT

Mix the garlic, ginger, lemon, oil and spices and marinate the chicken preferably overnight in the fridge.

Remove the chicken from the fridge to bring back to room temperature. Pre-heat the grill to high and when hot grill the chicken on foil until it is well coloured and even slightly charred before turning it over.

Once cooked through, turn off the grill and wrap the chicken in the foil to rest whilst you make the sauce. Slice the cucumber in four lengthways and cut into small ½ cm dice. Mix this with all the remaining sauce ingredients.

Toast the pitta bread and when warm, make a slit in the top so that you can open up the bread.

Put some sauce and lettuce in the pitta, pile in the chicken and spoon over more sauce. Eat immediately.

STICKY RIBS

There are so many different recipes for this. Marinating them definitely makes a difference - what you want is falls-off-the-bone, tender sweet meat. Style-wise, there are really two versions - Southern States Barbecue and Asian. I tend to hedge my bets with a hybrid!

Ribs are a fairly cheap cut of meat but not a great leftover. Also, I have never really found anything that really goes with them for me - and I have tried fries, potato skins, rice, coleslaw - I think they are generally so messy they just really need to be on their own. If you buy a whole rack of ribs, they will be easier to handle in the oven. Serving size truly depends on how piggy you are and whether you have any side dishes.

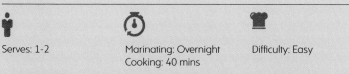

Serves: 1-2

Marinating: Overnight
Cooking: 40 mins

Difficulty: Easy

INGREDIENTS

Whole rack of pork ribs

4 dsp honey

6 dsp ketchup

6 dsp soy sauce

Small glass of orange juice

1 dsp marmalade

HOW TO MAKE IT

Mix all the ingredients and cover the ribs with the marinade. Cook the ribs at 180°C for an hour and a half, turning and basting frequently.

GARLIC BREAD

This really reminds me of being a student. If you have only ever experienced the shop bought one try this - it is so much yummier and contains garlic, butter, bread and herbs rather than the mono and di-glycerides of fat that are sometimes found in supermarket brands. Don't leave out the parsley, it will help you to digest the garlic.

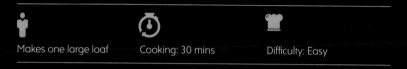

Makes one large loaf   Cooking: 30 mins   Difficulty: Easy

INGREDIENTS

One baguette - you may be able to buy a stale one cheaply from a bakery

3 fat cloves of garlic

100g softened butter

3 dsp chopped flat leaf parsley

HOW TO MAKE IT

Chop the garlic very finely, then add a large pinch of salt and keep chopping - the salt will almost melt the garlic. Mash this and the parsley into the butter with a fork.

Cut the baguette with even, diagonal slits, taking care not to cut through the bread. Spread the garlic butter into the slits and wrap loosely with foil. Bake at 200°C for 15 to 20 minutes.

VEGGIE...ISH

VEGGIE...ISH

It may have struck you that meat is relatively expensive. Fortunately, there are fantastic flavour and nutritional payoffs to eating vegetables and this chapter will give you some great building blocks.

If you are one of those sceptical people who have only experienced soggy, flavourless grey veggies, fear not - that particular world of pain can be put behind you now.

On the time front, one of the huge advantages of vegetables is that the cooking time is so short in comparison to meat - indeed there are a multitude of vegetarian meals that require little or no cooking at all.

Avocado, tomato and mozzarella salad. A jacket potato with grated cheese on the top. A simple salad of lettuce with a warm grilled disc of goat's cheese. All delicious suppers that can be produced quickly and with very little effort.

But variety is the spice of life, so you may want to try some of the following.

RISOTTO

The marvellous thing about risotto is that once mastered, you have an enormous potential for a variety of flavours and textures. Risotto is simply a dish of Italian rice- Carnaroli, Arborio or Vialone- that is coated in butter and then swelled slowly with stock. It never takes less than 20 minutes but it is a great option if you have very little to hand. You could make a delicious risotto with rice, butter, a stock cube and some parmesan cheese. Yet add some mushrooms or some prawns or peas and you have a different thing altogether. All you need to do is master the basic recipe and then let your imagination do the rest.

The first rule with risotto is that you are going to look at the amount of rice I am going to tell you to cook and think 'she has made a mistake, I am really hungry'. But I have tested this on a number of ravenous teenagers and this really should fill you up. Unlike most of the recipes in this book, I would advise against creating leftovers. Rice can contain a nasty little bacteria called Bacillus Cereus that can start its own growth industry if you do not chill the leftover risotto very rapidly. Unusually this bacteria cannot be destroyed by reheating so all in all, best to avoid the leftovers issue.

Serves: 1X   Cooking: 25 mins   Dfficulty: Easy as uno, due, tre

---

INGREDIENTS

150g risotto rice

400ml stock made up with a stock cube and boiling water in a saucepan

50g butter

50g grated parmesan cheese

HOW TO MAKE IT

Set the saucepan with stock on the hob on a very low simmer. Melt the butter in a wide-based pan over a medium heat as the wide base will help the rice cook evenly. Stir in the rice until it is completely coated in butter. Add a ladle full of stock to the rice and continue stirring until all the liquid has been absorbed.

Repeat until all the stock has been used up.

Taste the risotto. It will definitely need salt and pepper but if the rice is too al dente (it should have a bite to it rather than being complete baby food) you might need to add another ladle full of water.

If all is good with the rice, season, stir in half the parmesan and then serve in a bowl with the remaining parmesan.

That is about the most basic that you can make a risotto. You can pep it up no end by gently cooking finely sliced or diced shallot, onion, spring onion or celery in the butter until soft but not coloured and then adding the rice.

Little cubes of pancetta can be added to the pan and cooked through before stirring in the rice. You can also add mushrooms after the rice - the colour of the risotto will not be great but the taste will be and you can always lift the colour by adding some green herbs just before you serve the risotto.

Towards the end of the cooking time, with the last ladle of stock you can add some cooked chicken, some raw prawns, some taleggio cheese, some petits pois, a sliced courgette, steamed pumpkin or butternut squash.

At the very end of the cooking process, you can add in some freshly chopped herbs - chives work particularly well or the green ends of some spring onions. And mint is rather yummy with peas and/or prawns. A spoonful of crème fraîche or mascarpone cheese is good if you want some extra creaminess.

Go ahead and experiment but for me there are some things that just don't work. Tomatoes, beetroot, wine, carrots, cauliflower, corn, meat other than chicken and bacon - but that might just be me. You are aiming for something that adds flavour and/or texture and colour is a bonus too.

MUSHROOM SANDWICH

This is a brilliant wheeze, from Nigella Lawson via Nigel Slater.

Serves: 1X   Cooking: 25 mins   Difficulty: Easy

INGREDIENTS

1 enormous field mushroom

2 cloves of garlic, cut on a board and mashed with a sprinkling of salt

2 dsp finely chopped parsley

30g softened butter

Some Dijon mustard

Large roll, bap or baguette

HOW TO MAKE IT

Pre-heat the oven to 200°C. Work the garlic and parsley into the butter. Smear the butter over a large field mushroom and bake in your smallest oven-proof dish for about 20 minutes at 200°C.

Cut through a roll, small ciabatta, baguette, etc and use one side to mop up the juices in the pan and on the other side spread Dijon mustard.

Pop in the mushroom and voila. It's very delicious and curiously meaty, so great for vegetarians who crave the texture without the actual meat.

CAULIFLOWER CHEESE

This is a simple and satisfying meal. Make the cheese sauce from the macaroni cheese recipe on p.58 in the pasta chapter.

Serves: 2

Cooking: 40 mins

Difficulty: Easy

INGREDIENTS

1 whole cauliflower

50g butter

4 heaped dsp plain flour

1 litre milk

200g grated cheddar cheese

Nutmeg

A handful of breadcrumbs

HOW TO MAKE IT

Take a whole cauliflower and break off the florets. Slice the stalks into similar sized chunks as the florets. Tear off the leaves too.

Into a pan of boiling water place the stalks, followed a minute later by the florets.

After 5 minutes, add the leaves then a minute later, turn off the heat and drain. Arrange the cauliflower in a shallow dish and pour over the cheese sauce.

Scatter breadcrumbs on top and bake in an oven pre-heated to 180°C for 20 minutes.

WELSH RAREBIT

Very smart cheese on toast this:

Serves: 1X   Cooking: 10 mins   Difficulty: Easy

INGREDIENTS

Two large palmfuls of grated hard English (ironic, no?) cheese: Cheddar, Cheshire, Lancashire, etc

I egg yolk

½ tsp Colman's English mustard powder

Large splash of Worcestershire sauce

1 thick slice of bread

HOW TO MAKE IT

In order to separate an egg into yolk and white, crack the egg on the edge of a bowl at its widest (not longest) point so that the shell ruptures. Holding the egg upright over the bowl in your right hand-ease the lid off the egg with your left.

The egg white (clear when uncooked) will fall into the bowl and the yolk should remain in the shell. Tip the egg yolk gently into the shell in your left hand and this will allow more white to slip into the bowl. Repeat until you are left with only yolk.

The white can be covered and stored in the fridge and used within a few days to add to an omelette or scrambled eggs.

Pre-heat the grill. Mix all the ingredients except the bread together. Toast the bread on one side then spread the other side with the mixture. Grill until brown and bubbling.

Serve immediately.

BUBBLE
+ SQUEAK

Classically this is a dish composed of leftovers, but as a student I never seemed to have the right sort of leftovers and used to go and buy the fresh ingredients to create this dish. I expect that I did so because it is such warming comfort food and works brilliantly as a solitary supper. It is also much easier to form into patties when the components are still warm rather than cold from the fridge. The quantities are exceedingly elastic - there simply needs to be sufficient potato to hold together the carrot, cabbage and onion.

Serves: 4

Cooking: 30 mins

Difficulty: Easy

INGREDIENTS

If making from scratch:

4 large potatoes mashed (that is boiled until soft, then mashed)

2 grated carrots

2 handfuls of finely shredded cabbage

I finely chopped onion

HOW TO MAKE IT

Cook the onion in a small amount of butter until soft in the non-stick frying pan. Add in the cabbage and stir until it collapses.

Turn off the pan and tip it at an angle so that any fat can drain to one side. Spoon off the cabbage and onion into a bowl with the potato and carrot and mix thoroughly.

If the mixture is too dry and crumbly, add an egg. Form into tennis ball-sized shapes. Return the pan to the heat and once the fat has started bubbling, add a dessertspoon or two of oil and then the patty, now flattened to resemble a very generous hamburger.

Do not disturb for at least 5 minutes, then gently check the colour of the underside - it should be a deep golden brown, only just on the right side of burnt.

Once the desired colour has been reached, turn over and repeat. Finally balance on the side to cook the edges - there are four or maybe five. Geometrically unlikely but true!

There is your bubble and squeak patty. It is more traditional to just squash the lot into a frying pan, brown, turn over and keep repeating. This way produces undeniably delicious results but you need to add an artery blocking amount of fat to cook it. So I use the patty method.

If you have made more than you need, cook them all and wrap in foil and refrigerate to re-heat in the oven later in the week. They won't taste quite as good but good enough - just warm them through in an oven pre-heated to 180°C for about 20 minutes.

They will not freeze well as the potato will absorb too much water. You can bulk them up even further by putting a poached or fried egg on top. A rasher or two of bacon, a sausage or some poached smoked haddock also make particularly fine companions.

LOCAL
RED LEAF
LETTUCE
$1.25 EA

ITALY
ITALIAN FRISSE
$12.00 LB

Baby
Romaine
$10.00/LB

BABY Green
Oak Artisan
$8.00 LB

U.S
Baby Red
Artisan Oak
$8.00 LB

U.S
LITTLE
GEM LETTUCE
$4.00 LB

ITALIAN RADICCHIO
CASTILO FRANCO
$17.00 LB

ITALY
ITALIAN RADICCHIO
TREVISO
$.20.00 LB

U.S
BOSTON
Lettuce
$1.25 EA

HOW TO BUILD A SATISFYING SALAD

I know that this sounds like a load of pretentious old cobblers but it really does make a difference to how a salad looks and tastes if you assemble it with care.

That means thinking about the different textures, sizes, shapes, colours and flavours of the ingredients and how well they are going to sit on the same plate with each other. There are so many possible variations that it occurred to me that the choices could be presented like GCSE options.(see p.171)

I know that it seems a bit bonkers but I think that it works. You wouldn't need to use an ingredient from every column to make a decent salad- tomatoes and basil make a thoroughly nice dish as does lettuce and warm bacon. But I think that if you use this guide you can come up with a variety of extremely satisfying and vibrant combinations.

HERE ARE SOME EXAMPLES:

1	Spinach	1	Lettuce	1	Watercress
2	Quinoa	2	Tuna	2	Salmon
2	Feta	3	Potatoes	3	Peas
3	Peas	4	Green beans	4	Asparagus
4	Broccoli	5	Tomatoes	5	Fennel
5	Tomatoes	6	Eggs	6	Cucumber
6	Cucumber	7	Olives	7	Radishes
7	Alfalfa sprouts				

1	Spinach	1	Rocket	1	Spinach
2	Bacon	2	Lentils	2	Chicken
3	Croutons	4	Green beans	3	Wild rice
4	Mangetout	5	Red peppers	4	Sugar snap peas
5	Celery	6	Artichokes	5	Bean sprouts
6	Avocado	7	Chives	6	Butternut squash
7	Seeds			7	Cashews

INGREDIENTS

Select an ingredient from each column, though you can choose two from column 2 and leave out column 3 altogether. As far as quantity is concerned a small handful of each ingredient should do the trick. As you become better at cooking the balance will become more intuitive.

1. RAW

Lettuce / Rocket

Watercress

Spinach

4. BLANCHED

Broccoli

Green beans

Mangetout

Sugar snap peas

Asparagus

5. RAW

Tomatoes

Fennel

Celery

Peppers

Bean sprouts

2. COOKED

(apart from cheese)

Chicken

Prawn

Bacon

Tuna

Salmon

Goat's cheese

Feta cheese

Quinoa

Lentils

6. MISC.

Artichokes in oil

Avocado

Roasted butternut squash

Cucumber

Hard boiled eggs

Roasted beetroot

3. COOKED

(apart from peas)

Potatoes

Chickpeas

Rice (wild, red or black)

Croutons

Defrosted petits pois

7. RAW

Nuts

Seeds

Olives

Radishes

Sprouts, Alfalfa, etc.

Herbs

SUPERFOOD SALAD

The second salad in the examples (previous pages) you may recognise as the classic Nicoise.

I will give you a recipe for the first salad so that you have a better idea of what I mean by 'building' a salad. This salad is mainly inspired by the Leon superfood salad and it is utterly delicious, as well as being ridiculously good for you. It is just the sort of food to revive you when you are lacking in vitality. Add chicken or salmon or avocado if you feel the urge.

Serves: 1   Cooking: 25 mins   Difficulty: Easy

INGREDIENTS

A handful of:

Spinach leaves

Quinoa

Feta

Peas

Broccoli

Tomatoes

Cucumber

Alfalfa sprouts

HOW TO MAKE IT

Defrost a couple of palmfuls of frozen petits pois.

To prepare the broccoli, separate the florets into small evenly-sized pieces. Do not discard the stems as they are full of fibre and very tasty too! Drop the stems into a pan of boiling salted water, let it return to the boil, then add the florets. After no more than a few minutes test the broccoli - it should still be crunchy. Drain and refresh in cold water. In an ideal world you would plunge the broccoli into iced water but I doubt very much that you have that much ice, so cold water will have to do.

Quinoa (pronounced keen-wah) is an ancient American grain that is packed with protein, vitamins and minerals. It is more widely available than it used to be and you can pick it up at most supermarkets now. It is recognised as a superfood but don't let that put you off.

Whenever I cook some I make more than I need and then store it in the fridge to use to bulk up salads. A simple tomato salad will be much more filling if you add quinoa to it, for example. And according to a recent report, it is now cheaper than chips. To cook, rinse about 100g and then stir into a small pan of boiling water for 10 minutes, drain and return to the pan and leave until cooled.

Cut the tomatoes into bite-sized pieces.

Peel the cucumber so that it is stripy, cut in four lengthways and scoop out the seeds with a teaspoon. Cut across the lengths into 1 cm pieces.

Toss a couple of handfuls of spinach leaves in an oil and vinegar dressing. Lay half the leaves on the plate and then follow with layers of half of the quinoa, broccoli, cucumber, tomatoes, feta and peas. Dress with vinaigrette and then repeat. Finally sprinkle over the seeds and sprouts. My favourite dressing on this salad is one made with equal parts of maple syrup, olive oil and balsamic vinegar.

Eat this and you can almost feel the goodness seeping into your body.

COLESLAW

I have a fear of shop-bought coleslaw. It is invariably swimming in too much mayonnaise and the vegetables no longer have any bite to them. Eugh. It takes hardly any time or money to make a fresh, vibrant and crunchy slaw.

A cabbage goes a long way - so use up any leftovers for the bubble and squeak recipe earlier in the book.

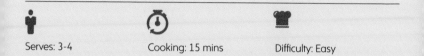

Serves: 3-4

Cooking: 15 mins

Difficulty: Easy

INGREDIENTS

½ finely shredded cabbage

3 sticks of celery, finely chopped

3 large carrots grated

A handful of raisins

2 very crunchy apples, thinly sliced

HOW TO MAKE IT

Mix all the ingredients except the apples together in a bowl.

In a separate bowl, mix 3 tbsp of mayonnaise with 4 tbsp vinaigrette (see dressings on p.176) and whisk together with a fork. Pour over the slaw and mix thoroughly. Then chop and add the apples. It is also nice with some seeds, especially pumpkin, for some added texture.

Coleslaw is brilliant with a jacket potato, a slice of ham, with bangers or burgers, or just on its own.

DRESSINGS

I have noticed that people get very twisted knickers when it comes to vinaigrette but really it is a question of what appeals to you and what you are dressing. And in the same way, that a bikini works well at the beach but not at a wedding, you need to dress appropriately for the occasion. Perfectly ripe tomatoes may be very happy with just some olive oil. More punchy structured leaves like Cos or Romaine can take a more robust dressing, whereas delicate ones like spinach or rocket can literally be drowned by something that is too weighty.

The dressing below works well on its own or mixed half and half with mayonnaise with a winter slaw of apples, celery, carrot and cabbage, though I would reduce the amount of sugar. The quantities are approximate and it is key that you make the dressing, leave it for 10 minutes or so then taste it using a lettuce leaf. It is pointless tasting it on a teaspoon unless you are planning on drinking it.

As far as the type of sweetener is concerned, you can use any number of things - sugar, honey, maple syrup, agave nectar or orange juice. Never discard the herby oil that is left over in jars of olives or artichokes or sun-dried tomatoes, as this is a brilliant and thrifty addition to your jar of dressing.

This recipe will make enough dressing for quite a few salads, so I would recommend putting it in a large screw-top jar. I never put mine in the fridge as I don't think that it does it any favours.

4 dsp Dijon mustard

4 dsp of sugar (optional)

150ml white wine or cider vinegar

1 tsp salt and a good grinding of pepper

300ml ground nut/sunflower/grape seed oil

300ml olive oil

If you want a joined up dressing, mix the first four ingredients and then slowly mix in the oil so that it emulsifies (such a lovely word - effectively in this case it means that the dressing joins up rather than separates) and season. If you prefer a separated out type thing, add all the ingredients into a jar and then shake. The oil will rise above the rest of the dressing.

If a milder-on-the-mustard-front dressing is your thing, replace the Dijon mustard with 2 dsp mustard powder. As much as I like to encourage experimentation, do not bother trying to use malt vinegar in a salad dressing, as the dominant flavour will obliterate rather than complement the taste of everything else.

Mixing equal parts of maple syrup, olive oil and balsamic vinegar together makes a good dressing for a salad with chicken, broccoli and squash.

RAINBOW ROASTED VEGETABLES

If you have a pile of roasted vegetables in the fridge, you will have many meal options.

Serves: 1X   Cooking: 1¼ hours   Difficulty: Easy

INGREDIENTS

Vegetables
Olive oil

HOW TO MAKE IT

Cut up a pile of raw vegetables - every colour peppers, red onions, fennel, squash, aubergines, sweet potatoes, courgettes, carrots. Leafy green or delicate vegetables will not take well to roasting, so best to avoid those. Toss in olive oil, season and roast on an oven tray at 200°C for 30 to 40 minutes until they are soft and slightly charred at the edges.

Now you have not only a meal in itself but also a pile of very versatile yumminess that can be added to salad leaves, pasta, rice, couscous, quinoa, made into a vegetable lasagne or scattered with some cheese (feta, taleggio) onto a piece of rolled out puff pastry and popped in the oven for 25 minutes at 180°C to make a tart.

WILD RICE + VEGGIES

I think that barely a week goes by in my house without this being made. It's not that my family has a low boredom threshold; it's the fact that the ingredients always vary, so the end result is never the same.

Invariably I start with an onion, shallot, spring onions or leeks but after that it could be almost anything - mushrooms, peppers, aubergines, squash, courgettes, spinach, broccoli. The rice I use has as much texture as possible - some supermarkets sell a mixture of wild, red and basmati rices that works well in this dish. I will give you a master recipe but please experiment away!

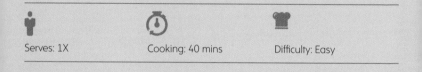

Serves: 1X   Cooking: 40 mins   Difficulty: Easy

INGREDIENTS

1 red onion, roughly chopped

1 yellow pepper, deseeded and diced

1 red pepper, deseeded and diced

250g mushrooms, sliced

A few cubes of frozen leaf spinach

I courgette sliced into thick one pound coins

125g rice

250ml stock

HOW TO MAKE IT

Sauté the onion in some olive oil in a non-stick wok until it is soft and browned, then add in the diced peppers. Stir in the rice followed by the mushrooms. Cook until the mushrooms have collapsed then add the stock and stir well.

Check the rice in 15 minutes and if it seems nearly cooked add in the spinach cubes and courgette. After 5 minutes turn the heat off and leave to settle for 5 minutes. Check the seasoning before serving.

You can add diced chicken thighs in after the onions, browning them on each side before adding the other ingredients. You will need a little more stock if you do so.

COLCANNON

For the times when being grown up and independent just feels hard and a long way from home, there is colcannon, a rather fine and rustic pile of Irish comfort food that is so much more than just mashed potato. It is not the most nutritious dish in this book, but you can't be angelic every day. Great on its own but scrumptious with a sausage, ham or a piece of fish.

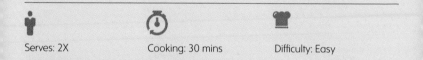

Serves: 2X

Cooking: 30 mins

Difficulty: Easy

INGREDIENTS

50g butter

5 spring onions, finely chopped

2 handfuls of shredded cabbage

2 large peeled potatoes, in cubes and boiled in salted water until soft

50ml milk

HOW TO MAKE IT

Drain the potatoes in their saucepan and keep warm with the lid on.

Melt the butter in a non-stick pan and slowly cook the spring onion until soft but not at all coloured. Add in the cabbage and cook until it softens.

Mash the potato in the saucepan with a fork. Add the milk to the spring onion/cabbage saucepan and when it is warm, add the potato and mix it all thoroughly with a fork. Taste, season and serve with an extra knob of butter.

BLACKENED SALMON IN MIRIN

This is the 'ish' in Veggie ish. This is loosely based on a dish in Nigella Express. I have given this to people who have never before liked salmon and they have devoured it. An added bonus is that salmon contain oils that are believed to be beneficial for your heart and brain.

Serves: 2X

Marinating: 30 mins
Cooking: 15 mins

Difficulty: Easy

INGREDIENTS

2 salmon fillets

4 dsp mirin

2 dsp brown sugar

4 dsp soy sauce

Thumb grated ginger

40ml rice wine

HOW TO MAKE IT

Mix the mirin, sugar, soy and ginger and marinate the salmon in that for at least half an hour.

In a hot non-stick frying pan dry-fry the salmon, non skin side down at first. Then turn the salmon and add the remainder of the marinade. It will bubble up quite a bit.

After about 5 minutes, remove the salmon to a warm plate, add 40ml of rice wine to the pan. Once the sauce has warmed through, pour over the salmon.

Serve with noodles and/or a green vegetable such as sugar snap peas or bok choi.

LEMON & GINGER RICE

This is adapted from a recipe from a fabulous chef called Reza Mahammed who is a sort of Anglo Indian Freddie Mercury with as much flair for performing. I am not sure about his musical prowess but he is a brilliant cook. I have included it because it will produce the most comforting, simple and delicious bowl of rice you will have ever tasted. If you get a cold, persuade someone to make this for you so that you can heal quicker. If you can't get hold of ghee don't fret - it was originally used in the recipe because it has a much higher smoking point than normal butter. So if you are using conventional butter just be careful that it doesn't burn in the last part of the recipe.

Serves: 6

Soaking: 30 mins
Cooking: 30 mins

Difficulty: Medium

INGREDIENTS

400g basmati rice

2 lemons' juice and zest

2 inch piece of ginger in julienne strips (think matchsticks)

1 tsp ghee (Hindi for clarified butter - in a tub from the supermarket) for the rice

Pinch turmeric

1 dsp ghee for tempering the seeds

l tsp mustard seeds

HOW TO MAKE IT

Wash the rice in a roomy bowl with hot water, drain and then wash it several times in cold water until the water is no longer cloudy with starch.

Then soak the rice in cold water and about 2 tbsp salt for at least 30 minutes. Drain into a sieve and rinse through the rice again with cold water by holding it under a tap. I know that this seems like a palaver but if you start off your rice cooking career like this, you will never have to suffer the unfortunate experience of gluey, overcooked yucky rice.

In a large saucepan with a tight fitting lid, combine 700ml water, the lemon juice and zest, half the ginger sticks, a good pinch of salt and the ghee.

Bring to the boil for a few minutes to allow the ginger to soften, then add the rice and turmeric.

Stir well to mix and then do not stir again. Once most of the liquid has evaporated and craters have started to appear on the surface, lower the heat to the absolute minimum.

Place a folded clean dry tea towel (locating one of these could be the most tricky part of the recipe) over the saucepan and then put on the lid. Leave for 10 minutes then remove from the heat. Do not lift the lid.

In a small frying pan, heat the ghee and as soon as it begins to smoke, add the other half of the ginger, stir-fry for a few minutes then add the mustard seeds and allow them to snap, crackle and pop. Lift the lid off the rice pan and add the tempered spices. Replace the lid, wash up the frying pan, by which time you can fork through the rice and serve.

INDEX